MACMILLAN MA

JOSEPH ANDREWS

BY HENRY FIELDING

TREVOR JOHNSON

**MACMILLAN
EDUCATION**

First edition 1987

Published by
MACMILLAN EDUCATION LTD
Houndmills, Basingstoke, Hampshire RG21 2XS
and London
Companies and representatives
throughout the world

Typeset in Great Britain by
TEC SET, Wallington, Surrey

Printed in Hong Kong

British Library Cataloguing in Publication Data

Johnson, Trevor, *1929* —
Joseph Andrews by Henry Fielding. —
(Macmillan master guides)
1.   Fielding, Henry. Joseph Andrews
I.   Title
823'.5   PR3454.J67
ISBN 0–333–40920–5 Pbk
ISBN 0–333–40921–3 Pbk export

CONTENTS

GENERAL EDITOR'S PREFACE

The aim of the Macmillan Master Guides is to help you to appreciate the book you are studying by providing information about it and by suggesting ways of reading and thinking about it which will lead to a fuller understanding. The section on the writer's life and background have been designed to illustrate those aspects of the writer's life which have influenced the work, and to place it in its personal and literary context. The summaries and critical commentary are of special importance in that each brief summary of the action is followed by an examination of the significant critical points. The space which might have been given to repetitive explanatory notes has been devoted to a detailed analysis of the kind of passage which might confront you in an examination. Literary criticism is concerned with both the broader aspects of the work being studied and with its detail. The ideas which meet us in reading a great work of literature, and their relevance to us today, are an essential part of our study, and our Guides look at the thought of their subject in some detail. But just as essential is the craft with which the writer has constructed his work of art, and this may be considered under several technical headings – characterisation, language, style and stagecraft, for example.

The authors of these Guides are all teachers and writers of wide experience, and they have chosen to write about books they admire and know well in the belief that they can communicate their admiration to you. But you yourself must read and know intimately the book you are studying. No one can do that for you. You should see this book as a lamp-post. Use it to shed light, not to lean against. If you know your text and know what it is saying about life, and how it says it, then you will enjoy it, and there is no better way of passing an examination in literature.

JAMES GIBSON

ACKNOWLEDGEMENT

Cover illustration: *Mr and Mrs Thomas Coltman* by Joseph Wright of Derby. Reproduced by courtesy of the Trustees, The National Gallery, London.

For Clement Clifford
'Toute passe, l'amitié resté.'

1 HENRY FIELDING: LIFE AND BACKGROUND

When he died in 1754, aged only 43, Henry Fielding was a highly respected magistrate, who had contributed greatly to the cleaning up of London's crime rings by helping to set up an effective police force. He was also a most successful novelist – still one of the select few whose works have never gone out of print. His last book *Amelia* (1751) earned him £880 (say £20,000 in today's currency but remember that a country gentleman could live well on £500 a year at the time). Yet his career in his early years, up to his first marriage in 1734, was anything but regular, respectable or even sober. So we must glance at his disturbed childhood and his wild youth, as well as his happy if tragically brief marriage, at the vein of profligacy as well as the powerful moral persuasions that grew on him in later life, if we are to understand the origins of that kaleidoscopic, by turns farcical, idyllic, brutal, sombre yet continually pulsating world which he created in *Joseph Andrews*.

Fielding's father was of good family, a brave and successful soldier in the Duke of Marlborough's army at the Battle of Blenheim and elsewhere who later became a General. He was also an improvident rakehell, a compulsive gambler who lost the equivalent of £15,000 at a sitting. His father-in-law actually cut him out of benefit from his daughter's inheritance, so that when Fielding's mother died in 1738, and Henry, the eldest child, was eleven, money was already tight. General Fielding promptly remarried, and, as he chose the impoverished, Roman Catholic Italian widow of a London eating-house proprietor, he offended at one stroke nearly all the conventions of his age and class. This action precipitated a bitter family quarrel in which Henry sided with his grandmother. She took him, with his brother and four sisters, into her home. She went to law, and won, over General Fielding's misappropriation of money left for the children's benefit. All this must have set up painful conflicts in the boy's mind.

He was now sent to boarding school, a sharp contrast with the peaceful rural surroundings of Somerset. Eton, his father's choice, was then barbaric, and he was often flogged, but his growing intellectual and physical strength – as an adult he was over six feet tall, powerful and quite fearless – enabled him to survive and even profit from a place which the poet Gray said 'no consideration upon earth' would ever persuade him to revisit, so that he left 'uncommonly versed in the classics.'

In part from that harsh upbringing, and in part from his reading of the Greek philosophers, derives that resilience, that stoicism in the face of pain and injustice which many characters in *Joseph Andrews* display. Later Fielding who was to suffer mental anguish, poverty, and ill-health in plenty, much of it self-inflicted, said that philosophy could 'elevate the mind and steel and harden it against the capricious invasions of fortune'. He was to need that support in due course, and it is a virtue that his characters, not all of them uniformly admirable, always display if they are to deserve any part of our sympathy. He never had any time for milksops like Didapper.

After attempting, at only 19, to improve his prospects by eloping with a pretty and only too willing heiress, he went up to London. Tall, handsome, hawk-nosed, with black, glittering eyes, full of vitality, charming and witty by turns, he was certainly susceptible to beauty, and beauty, it seems, was often susceptible to him. In his *Amelia* he gives us a snatch of autobiography, telling of a girl than whom '. . . it was impossible to conceive of a greater appearance of modesty, innocence and simplicity', despite which he had earlier seen her 'in bed with a rake at a bagnio (=brothel) smoking tobacco, drinking punch, talking obscenity and swearing and cursing . . .' This points us to a leading theme in *Joseph Andrews*. We are not to trust in appearances; the true nature of an individual does not derive from what they say or how they appear but only from their actions. The yawning gulf between things as they are and as they ought to be is a salient feature of his art.

His relationship with his father improved with time. But, though he had bed and food at home, to live in or on the fringes of London 'society' needed money. London 'society', in its own opinion, comprised around twelve hundred 'High people' as Fielding later came acidly to call them, out of a population of a quarter of a million. They had infinite leisure which they largely employed in intrigue, scandal, sex, drink, gambling and play-going, and also in displaying an infinite contempt for 'Low people'; practically everybody else, that is. But at the time Fielding was flattered to be 'accepted' and when his first play proved a hit (largely because it was what we now call a 'star vehicle') he embarked upon a career in which hurried, often slapdash writing kept him just on the right side of the debtors' prison door. He often wrote, it is said, on tobacco wrappers after a late night's drinking, but there are patches of crisp dialogue, farcical humour, acrid satire, and vivid topicality in all these plays. He already liked to 'send up' the pompous and pretentious. In his *Tom Thumb* he guys the absurd tragedies of his day with point and immense gusto. He also developed a vein of what we would now call 'black comedy'. When, in the superbly titled *Rape upon Rape* Constant – quite guiltless – is imprisoned, his gaoler tries to soft-soap him into sharing his room as follows:

CONSTANT: What is the cause of his misfortune? [i.e. the other prisoner's]
STAFF: A rape, Captain, a rape – no dishonourable offence – I would not have brought any scoundrel into your honour's company, but rape and murder no gentleman need be ashamed of, and this is an honest brother ravisher.

This assumption that everyone shares their own depravity is a hallmark of the villains in *Joseph Andrews*, of course, and simultaneously comic and corrective. The plays soon moved into the dangerous area of political satire. When Fielding put Walpole (Prime Minister from 1721 to 1742) on stage as *Mr Quidam* (*quidam* = a certain person), first 'convincing' the 'patriots' by throwing gold to them and then playing the fiddle so that they all dance off to his tune, the point was taken at once by the man who, pointing to the House of Commons, had said 'All these men have their price'. Theatrical censorship by the Lord Chamberlain's office was instituted in 1737, and left Fielding, who had rashly invested in theatre management too, with no means of supplementing his income from 1737. But what was much worse than his own predicament was that of his wife and young family.

For Fielding had married in 1734, and though his wife, Charlotte Cradock brought some money with her it was soon squandered. As a near contemporary put it:

He loved her passionately and she returned his affection, yet had no happy life. For they were seldom in a state of quiet and safety. All the world knows what was his imprudence; if he possessed a score of pounds [say £400 today] nothing could keep him from lavishing it idly, or make him think of the morrow.

Now, driven by love, compassion and need, Fielding began to study the law, simultaneously editing (and largely also writing) a periodical called *The Champion*. This contains, piecemeal, a good deal that looks forward to the novels. He warmly commends the great painter Hogarth 'in whose excellent works you see the delusive scene exposed with all the Force of Humour . . .', a phrase equally apposite to his own *Joseph Andrews*. But the incessant strain of study and writing, of penny-pinching and caring for his now ailing wife began to damage even his powerful physique. Thus, when he was called to the bar in 1740, and had to give up journalism as incompatible with his new profession, his income from the law, for which he had qualified in half the usual time of six years by superhuman efforts, was small and precarious.

There was then no system of 'social security', no 'health insurance'. medicine was in its infancy, perhaps as few as one child in ten saw maturity, and, even for the wealthy, debt, degradation, and starvation were ever-present threats if they made the wrong investments.

So, when we read *Joseph Andrews*, we shall do well to remind ourselves that its extreme vagaries of fortune, its brutality, monstrous injustices, its evidences of hunger, dirt, ignorance, exploitation and unbridled rapacity are not figments of Fielding's overheated imagination. On the contrary, they were, to his contemporaries, instantly recognisable as components of the everyday scene. It was against a background of grief, illness and painfully acquired experience that Fielding compiled his novel to be a testimony to human values as opposed to inhuman calculation, as exemplified in creatures like Peter Pounce. *Joseph Andrews* is a triumphant assertion of laughter's power to temper adversity and drive out despair, but it is, of course, more than this. Though never serious in the sense of glum or dry, it has much wisdom to offer, wisdom of an often 'disarmingly simple' kind, as Martin Battestin has said.

Fielding laid no claim to be a philosopher. He was, however a convinced and active Christian of that party in the Anglican Church of his day which took the pragmatic view that Man was capable of helping himself a good deal without Divine intervention at every turn, and that it was his duty to help his neighbour (in the sense of alleviating his distress) whenever possible. When Mrs Tow-wouse says 'Charity a fart!' she is, in Fielding's view, saying something literally damnable. Fielding, like many of the clergy of his day, profoundly distrusted the 'salvation by grace alone' position. It was not that he thought there was no need for faith in Christianity, rather that he accepted St Paul's placing: 'And now abideth these three; Faith, Hope and Charity. And the greatest of these is Charity' (i Corinthians, 13) in a literal sense. For Charity, in the sense of Love or Loving Kindness, is to Adams, as plainly it is to his creator, the acid test of a man's belief. 'Preaching and praying' alone, are of no use, says Adams, and goes on to horrify the orthodox Barnabas by contending that '. . . a virtuous and good Turk . . . is more acceptable in the sight of his Creator . . . than a vicious and wicked Christian'.

But if Fielding was convinced of the overriding need for us to behave lovingly, he certainly did not subscribe to the view that the world was one vast illustration of God's beneficence, properly understood; nor could he accept such facile optimism as was served up by Pope (in his *An Essay on Man*, 1733–4), for example

> God sends not Ill; if rightly understood
> [Our] partial Ill is Universal Good . . .

or

> One Truth is clear, WHATEVER IS, IS RIGHT!

On the contrary, as a metropolitan magistrate used to 'raking in the lowest sinks of iniquity', as one of his contemporaries, Lady Montagu, put it, he could not have failed to be aware of a world, to borrow a phrase from Dr Johnson again, 'bursting with sin and misery'. He did not despair; he did his best himself to try to alleviate some of the worst of the effects of poverty, but he was unable to rationalise it all away. Though ultimately he put his trust in Providence he saw no cause to abandon common sense. He was a reasonable man but one who distrusted reason deployed without belief. His most despicable characters are dab hands at using sophistry to defend their indefensible conduct.

So, in *Joseph Andrews*, it will not be hard to see Fielding's convictions at work. We must be careful to distinguish between them and the views aired by his characters; not difficult to do as a rule, except that we need to be cautious about supposing that *everything* Adams says would have Fielding's entire concurrence. Adams is a man, and men are fallible creatures, capable, all the same, of redeeming themselves. That is a concept central to Christianity, as it is to *Joseph Andrews*.

Fielding's finances were not greatly improved by *Joseph Andrews*, for which he received £185 from his publisher, Millar. One year later, however, he issued his *Miscellanies*. These three volumes of his journalism also contained the brilliant and ferocious short satirical novel *Jonathan Wild* in which a once-famous criminal is celebrated, tongue-in-cheek throughout, as a 'Great Man'. He earned £700 from the *Miscellanies*, but only one year later his wife Charlotte, whom he adored, died suddenly, prostrating him with grief. Two years later, in 1747, he married Mary Daniel, his wife's devoted maidservant and nurse, who had cared for his children after Charlotte's death. He was indifferent to the mockery of those who thought he had married 'beneath' him, and his appointment as Justice of the Peace for Westminster (a permanent salaried appointment as stipendiary magistrate) in 1748, gave him some security at last.

In 1749 he published his masterpiece, *The History of Tom Jones, a Foundling*, in six volumes, one of the dozen or so greatest novels in the English language. This brought him fame and provoked controversy, besides giving his finances a useful shot in the arm. He published a number of pamphlets aimed at reforming social and criminal abuses. One, his *Enquiry into the Causes of the Late Increase of Robbers*, was instrumental in helping towards the setting up, by his brother the famous blind Justice John Fielding, of the Bow Street Runners, the first effective professional police force in Britain.

He was by now well known, both as author and as a stern but just and quite incorruptible magistrate. His new novel, *Amelia*, a more serious work than the others, was eagerly awaited and, financially, a huge success, though it has not lasted as well as its predecessors. He had suffered for some time from the gout, a painful and immobilising scourge of the eighteenth century. Now it turned to dropsy, and in search of relief in a warmer climate, he set sail for Lisbon, in Portugal on 7 August, 1754. He confronted the agonising rigours of the voyage with wit and humour, recording them in his last book *Journal of a Voyage to Lisbon*, published posthumously only a few months after his death (in Lisbon) on 8 October 1754. Almost the last words he wrote, in a 'coffee house . . . pleasantly situated on the brow of a hill, [with] a very fine prospect of the river Tajo (Tagus) to the sea' were:

'Here we regaled ourselves with a good supper, for which we were as well charged as if the bill had been made on the Bath-road, between Newbury and London.' (The Bath Road, over which innumerable stage-coaches ran, was noted for its high prices.) There, undiminished, are the keen eye for the passing scene, the delight in the good things of life, and the mordant humour which had served him so well in *Joseph Andrews*.

2 INFLUENCES

2.1 THE NOVEL IN ENGLAND BEFORE FIELDING

Prose fiction had enjoyed quite a long history in England, and a much longer one in Europe, before Fielding's day. The origins of what we now call novels are Italian. Freely translated into English during the sixteenth and seventeenth centuries, these *novella storia* (i.e. *new stories*) are lively, ingenious and often vulgar tales, so that the title *novel* came to be associated with bawdy, disreputable work. Fielding only employs it once, dismissively. On the other hand *romance* (from the French *roman*), which he prefers, had by the mid-eighteenth century, acquired overtones of wild implausibility and high-flown sentiment. Indeed, Fielding speaks disparagingly in *The Author's Preface* of 'those voluminous works called romances [which contain] very little instruction or entertainment.'

Why then does Fielding happily christen his book a '*Comic Romance*', since he can hardly have been unaware of this shift in attitude? It is because as he acknowledges in his sub-title, he wrote '*in imitation of the manner of Cervantes, author of Don Quixote*'. This was the first and remains one of the very greatest European novels. Written in 1605 and completed in 1615 it was almost immediately translated into English. Its knightly hero, on his ungainly horse Rosinante, accompanied by his reluctant and sardonic 'squire' Sancho Panza, has passed into popular myth (see the dictionary under '*quixotic*') as he tilts at the windmills which he takes for giants and elevates a homely inn-keeper's daughter into a Queen of Hearts. But though the book began as a debunking attack upon the interminable romances with which Don Quixote has stuffed his head until he cannot distinguish fact and fiction, it soon turns into an indictment of those people who, in deriding Don Quixote, reveal their own lack of any ideals whatsoever, who are indeed devoted to money-grubbing and self-aggrandisement without risk. So Don Quixote's death is ultimately both tragic and uplifting.

It is easy to see that Parson Adams is a lineal descendant of Don Quixote, with his, sometimes woolly, idealism, his courage, his proneness to mockery and misadventure, his readiness to believe the best of everyone, his indifference to external appearances, his passion for reading, and so on. But this is not the moment to analyse in detail what Fielding meant by '*imitating the manner*' of Cervantes. For the time being it is enough to acknowledge a substantial debt, but not to exaggerate its importance.

A much less significant influence was the *picaresque* novel (from the Spanish *picar* = rogue). These all relate the exploits of what we might call anti-heroes and their intermittently successful flouting of society and its laws. Although Fielding does warmly commend one of the most famous, Le Sage's *Gil Blas of Santillana* (1715), the *picaresque* element in Joseph Andrews is minimal and confined to one aspect. Because rogues who stay put are apt to get caught *picaresque* plots essentialy consist of – often rapid – journeys. This is true of *Joseph Andrews*, obviously (just as it is of *Don Quixote*). But there the resemblance ends because, whereas picaresque 'heroes' are, to put it mildly, morally ambiguous, full of deceit, lies and trickery, we are never left in any doubt whatever in *Joseph Andrews* as to what is the morally right course of action, or whether Fielding's heroes will take it, whether or not it is expedient or advantageous.

Daniel Defoe's is probably the best claim to be the founding father of the English novel. But, apart from his famous *Robinson Crusoe* (1719) – which had its origins in a true shipwreck – Defoe's works are all very much in the *picaresque* line. Thus his heroine, *Moll Flanders* (1722) is described in Defoe's sub-title as 'borne in Newgate [prison], ten year a whore, three times married (once to her own brother), a transported felon . . .', and so on. If Fielding read Defoe, and I know of no evidence that he did, then the influence was a negative one. For Defoe's novels are, without exception, pseudo-autobiographies, told in the first person with such consummate skill that the critic Leslie Stephen once remarked that 'Defoe . . . lies like the truth'. He was so successful that some of his inventions were cited as historical documents until well into the nineteenth century. Fielding would have nothing to do with this, as he saw it, confidence trick. Pseudo-autobiography, persuading the reader that the tale must be true because the teller was there and saw it happen was not to be his way of writing a novel. On the contrary he quite deliberately and consistently disengages himself from his narrative, inviting us to share in the creator's bird's-eye or God's-eye view of his creations. This is a great leap forward in the history of the novel, enabling it to come of age, to stand on its own feet as it were, freed from the need to masquerade as a slice of life. What we have seen so far of the history of the novel reveals two positive influences on Fielding – Cervantes and, though of less significance, the *picaresque* novels. But it was not Defoe who prompted Fielding to abandon the first person narrative. It was Samuel Richardson (1689–1761), whose work was so crucial an influence upon Fielding's, albeit almost entirely a negative influence, that he must be treated separately.

2.2 SAMUEL RICHARDSON, *PAMELA*, *SHAMELA*, AND THEIR INFLUENCE ON *JOSEPH ANDREWS*

It is not going too far to say that, but for Richardson's having published, and enjoyed a runaway success with, *Pamela or Virtue Rewarded* in 1740, we should not have had *Joseph Andrews* at all, or not in anything like its present shape at least. It is indisputably the catalyst which set up a creative ferment in Fielding's mind. We must therefore have at least a rudimentary notion of what *Pamela* is about, and why it affected Henry Fielding so radically that he twice let fly at it in print. Richardson was a prosperous London printer and book-seller – really more like what we call a publisher – when he was invited, in 1739, to compile a series of *Familiar Letters*, as a sort of Augustan agony aunt's guide for, as he put it, 'handsome girls . . . obliged to go out to [domestic] service . . . on how to avoid the snares that might be laid against their virtue'. He began, but dropped this project in favour of a novel in the *epistolary* form (i.e. written as a series of letters) prompted by his 'recollection' of a real servant-girl who had won her would-be seducer to marry her by her 'noble persistence, watchfulness and excellent qualities'

As Richardson tells it, Pamela is hardly typical of eighteenth-century serving maids of 15. She has to be 'conspicuously literate' since she writes nearly all the letters herself, undaunted by the interception of her mail by the agents of her employer and per-secutor, the ominously anonymous 'Squire B' (whose name Fielding hilariously seized on and expanded to Booby, of course). Pamela, who formerly worked for his dead mother, is first abducted and then virtually imprisoned by him. Her one ally, the virtuous Parson Williams, is gaoled by Squire B on a trumped-up charge, and the Squire then makes repeated, if ineffectual, attempts on her 'virtue', culminating in the scene where he disguises himself as another servant-girl, gets into bed with Pamela and the odious Mrs Jewkes, who helps him pin her down and eggs him on to violate her. At this point 'With struggling and terror I fainted away . . . so that they both thought me dying', writes Pamela.

This is the emotional watershed, Squire B is now progressively worn down by Pamela's 'surpassing goodness', not to mention her obduracy. He at first proposes to instal her as his paid-up mistress and then offers her marriage, which, after she has at first rejected him on the grounds that it would be a 'sham ceremony' – excusably in the circumstances – she accepts. Here the interest, though not the book, ends, with the wedding and an orgy of sentimental forgiveness all round; even the appalling Mrs Jewkes finds favour with Pamela. There are, to be sure, another 150 pages of Pamela's progress as the lady of a great household, and – after imitations had vexed him – Richardson wrote an ill-judged sequel. But it was primarily the part I have summarised that attracted Fielding's attention, and, after he had read it and heard the gushing encomiums pronounced on it from pulpit and drawing-room alike, prompted him to express his mingled anger and amusement, initially in a short *parody* (i.e. a mocking imitation) called *Shamela*, and later in the opening sequences of *Joseph Andrews* whose hero is, of course, Pamela's brother and whose original employer was the uncle of Pamela's husband, Sir Thomas Booby.

Shamela

It is not hard to see what amused Fielding, who was anyway a much more sophisticated, wordly-wise and hard-boiled reader than most, in *Pamela*. First is the implausibility of the brutal and licentious Squire B's reformation. Men like him, in Fielding's experience, would either have debauched or sacked Pamela in double quick time, while only a fool would have married someone so far below him in 'rank'. Then Richardson cannot avoid the risible spectacle of the 'modest' Pamela cataloguing her own excellences, while the deliberately 'artless' style he uses for her often verges on the ludicrous. Cascades of 'O's' run down the page and she resorts to italics (what would have been underlinings) at every opportunity. But perhaps the most implausible event is the transformation of Squire B from toad into Prince Charming in what is, after all, not a fairy-tale.

If this were all, Fielding might well have been content to laugh up his sleeve. But, as we have seen, he held strong views on morality in action.

If *Pamela* were to be taken seriously as advice, Fielding thought, it would need to advocate morality in the full sense, not, as it appeared to do, in the highly restricted sense which identifies virtue with virginity. Fielding does indeed mock at Pamela's inordinate attachment to the word, which in *Shamela* he makes her spell *vartue* (as it was then pronounced), but the crucial point is that, as Fielding might have said, 'all virgins are not virtuous nor all the virtuous virgins'. The practical effect, says Parson Oliver (who speaks for Fielding in *Shamela*) is merely to encourage servant-girls ' . . . to look out for their master as sharp as they can', or, as we should say, 'to have a keen eye for the main chance.' As Parson Oliver also observes, Richardson is himself, for all his repeated condemnation of it, fascinated by sex, and thus, however unintentionally, contrives to produce some pretty suggestive scenes. So that Fielding felt

Richardson laid himself open to attack on two counts, as writer and as lay preacher, and attacked on both fronts accordingly.

Shamela is one of the most devastating parodies in English, funny even if one hasn't read the original. It is quite short, wickedly pointed, often bawdy though never smutty, grossly unfair of course, and stylistically speaking, it brilliantly catches Richardson's manner, which was designedly naive anyway, so that Fielding had a perfect target for mockery. Martin Battestin's edition of *Joseph Andrews* (see Further Reading) includes the whole of *Shamela*, which can easily be read in an hour or two.

3 SUMMARIES AND CRITICAL COMMENTARY

3.1 OVERALL SUMMARY OF THE PLOT

Book I

After giving us succinct character sketches of Joseph himself, the Reverend Abraham Adams, and Lady Booby's factotum, Mrs Slipslop, Fielding relates how, after Squire Booby's death, his widow, Lady Booby, first promotes the handsome Joseph to be her footman, and then takes him to London with her, where he picks up some of the airs and graces of city servants but twice spurns Lady Booby's determined attempts to seduce him. Egged on by Mrs Slipslop, whose cruder advances he has also rejected, she angrily dismisses him, and he sets out, at night, to walk home. He is set upon by footpads and after a gallant defence is robbed, stripped naked, and left for dead. The occupants of a passing stage-coach reluctantly convey him to an inn where he is grudgingly accommodated and visited, to no avail, by the doctor and the local vicar. There Adams, who has set off to London in hopes of selling his sermons, finds him in bed. Joseph's inherent toughness soon overcomes his injuries and the friends decide to resume their journeys. An animated discussion at dinner is interrupted by a furious row between the landlord and his wife, the terrifying Mrs Tow-wouse, who has discovered her husband in bed with Betty the chambermaid, she having, like Lady Booby, first failed in her efforts to seduce the incorruptible Joseph. The hullabaloo, and Book I, end with Betty's dismissal.

Book II

Joseph discovers that Adams has left his sermons behind, so they both set off homewards, intending to 'ride and tie' (see Fielding's explanation, Book II, Ch.2). After Adams's departure Joseph, detained because he cannot pay for the horse's feed, is released by Mrs Slipslop who has arrived by coach from London. While Joseph walks on, the passengers are told the story of Leonora (the first of Fielding's four 'digressions'). At the next inn Adams, whom they have now overtaken, fights the landlord for his cruelty to Joseph, who has injured his leg, lays him out, and is drenched with hogsblood by the landlord's wife, whom Mrs Slipslop then sets about. Peace restored, the coach proceeds with Joseph now inside, and the tale of Leonora is concluded. They now see, but cannot catch up with, Adams (who has, of course, forgotten his horse again and in racing the coach loses himself too). He encounters a sportsman, to whom he relates part of his life-story. His new acquaintance, who has repeatedly vaunted his own courage, promptly runs away when they hear a scream, leaving Adams to rescue a young woman from a rapist, whom he knocks out after a fierce fight, but who slyly – when some wayfarers arrive – claims that Adams and Fanny (as the young woman proves to be) are robbers who attacked *him*. They are all hauled off to the ignorant local JP and Adams can only establish their innocence when he is, by chance, recognised as a clergyman. He sets off with Fanny, and they are soon reunited with Joseph, at an inn, to their great delight. But they have no money and Adams's efforts to borrow from the pig-like Parson Trulliber prove abortive, though an impoverished pedlar is more generous and relieves them. At the next alehouse they meet the squire who promises them horses for the next day. But, as is his unpleasant habit, he lets them down so that they set off again on foot.

Book III
The first part of the Book is taken up by the travellers' encounter with the hospitable Mr Wilson, whom they meet after an unnerving walk in the dark. He tells them his life-story, something of a rake's progress. Next day, when they are resting, they are attacked by the hounds from a neighbouring hunt, whose master invites them to stay. First verbal insults are heaped then practical jokes are played upon Adams at dinner. He responds in kind and he, Joseph and Fanny leave in haste. They are pursued and captured by the squire's henchmen whose leader, the captain, takes Fanny away with him, leaving Joseph and Adams behind, and tied up. But she, and they, are set free by Mr Peter Pounce, Lady Booby's steward and all set out for the Booby estate together.

Book IV
The now returned Lady Booby still has her eye on Joseph. After hearing their banns called in church she tries to browbeat Adams into preventing the match between Joseph and Fanny and, when he indignantly refuses, employs Lawyer Scout to have them arrested on a trumped-up charge. But Lady Booby's nephew, Squire Booby, has just come visiting with his new wife (née Pamela *Andrews*) and he naturally cannot have his brother-in-law imprisoned. The justice defers to him and frees the lovers, only for new objections to be raised to the marriage on the ground that Joseph will now be

marrying 'beneath' him. He rejects this advice, at which Lady Booby attempts to promote an affair between Beau Didapper, one of her guests, and Fanny, who detests him at sight. However, the pedlar Adams had borrowed from (in Book II) returns to claim his debt, and gives what appears to be irrefutable evidence that Fanny is really Joseph's sister, stolen in her infancy by gipsies and bought from them by Sir Thomas Booby (now dead), who commissioned the Goodwills to bring her up as their own child. This revelation delights some and appals others of the company, who all stay the night at Booby Hall where various farcical mishaps involve Didapper, Slipslop, Joseph, Adams and Fanny. Next day, the Andrews arrive and, faced with the news from the pedlar, Mrs Andrews attests that, whereas Fanny is indeed her daughter, Joseph is *not* her son, but a baby who was abandoned by the same gipsies who stole Fanny, an 'exchange' she concealed from her husband, then abroad in the army. The opportune arrival of Mr Wilson (who had entertained Adams, Fanny and Joseph in Book III, Chs 2–3) as Joseph's unusual birthmark is mentioned, reveals Joseph as his son. All impediments removed, Lady Booby and the ill-disposed balked, the lovers marry, Mr Booby confers a good living on Adams, and they live happily, far removed from 'high-life'.

3.2 CHAPTER SUMMARIES AND CRITICAL COMMENTARY

Note. The chapters of *Joseph Andrews* are mostly so short (on average three to four pages only) that it would be tedious to deal with them one at a time. I have therefore divided the Books into 'episodes' which have internal coherence.

Author's Preface

Summary
Fielding intends to write a 'comic romance' or 'comic epic' in prose, a work wholly different from those lengthy, and – he believes – dull and pointless 'romances' his readers are only too familiar with. His book will be light-hearted in mood, will accordingly contain varied scenes from 'low' as well as 'high' life, and, while avoiding the 'monstrous and grotesque' will at times employ *burlesque* (i.e. 'sending up', as we should say, the overblown phrasing of 'serious' works by exaggerating it to the point of absurdity). He will nevertheless draw his characters from real life, without deviating from 'nature' (i.e. 'the general inherent character or disposition of mankind') because 'life everywhere furnishes an accurate observer with the ridiculous'. Comedy, as his own work for the stage has proved to him, can produce through 'exquisite mirth and laughter' a highly beneficial

effect upon the mind, something he hopes to achieve, like Hogarth in painting, by creating believable portraits rather than 'monsters'.

Accordingly, he will concentrate, not on the cheap success obtainable by depicting the deformed or pitiful personality, but on those who are made ridiculous by their 'affectation' (i.e. their pretence to good qualities they do not practice). Such affectation has many forms but only two sources; vanity and hypocrisy, of which hypocrisy is the more absurd and hence deserving of ridicule, because the hypocrite *knows* he is the opposite of what he pretends to be. If it is objected that he depicts vice he would argue that truth demands its inclusion, and that he never applauds it or allows it to triumph finally. No real person is depicted, and the most 'glaring' (i.e. prominent) character, Adams, though he appears in undignified episodes, displays such 'perfect simplicity' (i.e. total guilelessness or innocence) that he is really a model of what a clergyman ought to be in essentials.

Commentary

This is close-packed, argumentative, formally phrased, and, to a modern reader, rather dry stuff. But it is quite central to an understanding of the novel, since not only does it tell us *what* Fielding was trying to, but also, in part, *why* and *how* he proposes to do it. Fielding also felt he must disarm potential critics, as he was attempting to break new ground with a readership drawn from the tiny literate minority (perhaps fifty to sixty thousand out of a total population of six million or so). Even those who *could* read were largely unsophisticated in taste, and accustomed, if they read novels (which could easily be thought corrupting anyway) to sloppier sentiment, high-flown windy speeches and remorselessly rubbed in 'morals', or, alternatively to the wildest flights of fantasy. Perhaps two sentences should be learnt by heart, since they underscore the movement of the entire book; almost every incident either exemplifies or comments upon one or the other. The first is 'Life everywhere furnishes an accurate observer with the ridiculous'; and the second, which qualifies the first, is: 'The only true source of the ridiculous . . . is affectation.'

Fielding's success in achieving his aims is best attested by Dr Samuel Johnson (who much preferred Richardson's novels and is therefore a good witness). In *The Rambler*, No. 4 (this was a literary periodical), only eight years after *Joseph Andrews* had appeared, he asserted that 'the present generation' was tired of 'machines . . . giants . . . knights . . . castles . . . deserts' and so on. Novelists must now display that 'experience [arising] from general converse and accurate observation of the world' which will enable their works to serve as 'lectures of conduct and introductions into life'. Which is pretty much what Fielding had claimed in his *Preface*.

Book I

Chapters 1–3. Summary

The first chapter is really an extension of the Preface. It begins with a tongue-in-cheek commendation of 'biographies' of 'great and worthy' persons, exemplified by such far-fetched fairy tales as *Jack and the Beanstalk*. It then mockingly commends the recent 'lives' of Colley Cibber and Pamela Andrews, for their 'good example' of first male and then female virtue. His own 'authentic history' will show, Fielding says, not only how Joseph has profited from his sister's example, but will also display the only virtue (chastity), which Colley Cibber does not commend to his readers.

Chapters 2–3 introduce Joseph who was 'esteemed' (i.e. supposed) to be the son of Gaffar and Gammar Andrews (the names indicate old age). He is the brother of the 'famous' Pamela. His ancestry is obscure, but, having learned to read and write, he is, at ten years old, apprenticed to Sir Thomas Booby, the local squire, where he works his way up from bird-scarer to jockey. He excels at riding, being skilful, courageous, and unbribable. Lady Booby takes favourable notice of him and makes him her footboy when he is seventeen. His good behaviour, modest demeanour and fine singing voice bring him to the attention of the curate, Mr Abraham Adams, when he attends Lady Booby to church.

Adams is very learned, speaks many languages, is perceptive, accomplished and warmhearted but totally unworldly, 'Simplicity' (i.e. ingenuousness) is his 'characteristic,' he is grave, generous and believes the best of everyone. He lives, with difficulty, on a stipend of £23 a year, on which he supports a wife and six children.

Adams is so impressed by Joseph's knowledge of the Bible and other books, by his modesty and contentment with his station in life, that he wishes to help him. However, as Sir Thomas and Lady Booby are at loggerheads with the parson (Adams's nominal superior) he can only approach them via Mrs Slipslop, Lady Booby's housekeeper companion. This conceited person has some respect for Adams because she was a curate's daughter, but she is vain of her own learning, which she employs to mangle the English language, and Adams fails in his attempt to persuade her to intercede with Lady Booby, so that Joseph may be put in Adams's care to further his education.

Commentary

Chapter 1 opens with such dead-pan seriousness that we take it for a sincere commendation of 'biography' as 'improving' until, in the third paragraph Fielding reveals that he has been stringing us along by giving, as examples, the kind of books that cheapjacks sold for a penny, door-to-door. It is a little like saying today that *The Beano* will 'sow the seeds of virtue in youth'. This prepares the ground for his digs at Cibber and Richardson. The first, in his immensely popular *An Apology for His Life* (1740) had insulted Fielding, who now strikes back by praising the book for just those qualities it notoriously lacks: modesty and innocence (at this defect he once again snipes in Chapter 3). The second author is slyly mocked for his use of several nauseatingly fulsome letters of praise – what we should call blurbs – as a preface to the second edition of *Pamela*.

Chapters 2 and 3

An Epic, comic or otherwise, ought to start *in medias res* (i.e. 'in the middle of things') so Fielding is perforce economical in his sketches of the three principal characters without some knowledge of whom we cannot begin. The second paragraph of Chapter 3 provides a fine specimen of Fielding's mastery of sardonic or sub-acid tone. Notice the italicised words in these, at first glance quite innocent, phrases: ' . . . had *so much endeared and commended* him to a bishop, that *at the age of fifty*, he was provided with a *handsome* income *of twenty-three pounds a year*; which however, *he could not make any great figure with*, because he . . . was a *little encumbered* with a wife and six children'. This acrid irony is one of Fielding's prime weapons in his war on affectation. It is so important, and so frequently recurring, a feature of his work that, in this typical example, it may be useful to paraphrase literally what Fielding is *really* saying, what he *means*. In effect, '*Adams's outstanding claims to be promoted were matters of such indifference to the bishop that, long after preferment should have come his way, he was given a miserable pittance on which he could barely keep himself and his family*'. It is easy to miss Fielding's often savage criticisms unless we learn to recognise the caustic understatement, the refusal to tear a passion to tatters, which is his hallmark. Mrs Slipslop's blunders with long words are a less successful form of humour.

Chapters 4–10. Summary

Although, after his arrival in London, Joseph takes up the fashions popular among footmen to some degree, dressing himself impeccably and becoming an arbiter of musical taste, he remains unaffected by the temptations to drink, swear and gamble. However, his handsome appearance and gentlemanly bearing further attract Lady Booby's interest, and her familiar behaviour towards him does occasion some gossip. This is unjustified, but, after her husband's sudden death, which leaves her quite unmoved, she promptly contrives an opportunity to attempt the seduction of Joseph (as Fielding now elects to call him). He is at first too innocent and then too virtuous to respond to her innuendoes. In a rage compounded of guilt and frustration, Lady Booby dismisses him.

Joseph, in a letter to Pamela his sister (who is still having *her* virtue besieged by young Mr Booby at this time) confides that he thinks his mistress is 'mad' and that he wishes to return home as he dislikes London. The amorous and amoral Mrs Slipslop offers him tea and sympathy, not to mention her own dubious charms, but he repels her and also offends her vanity by likening her to his mother. Nevertheless, she is about to attempt a direct assault upon his virtue when she is summoned to Lady Booby's presence to discuss Joseph's future. Desiring to ingratiate herself with her mistress, and piqued anyway by Joseph's indifference to her attractions, she claims that he is a lecher who has, among others, seduced Betty, the chambermaid. Lady Booby, enraged by this, orders both of them to be dismissed, but after some shilly-shallying, and urging by Slipslop, reprieves Joseph.

After Fielding, by way of preparation, has given a rather luscious account of Joseph's masculine attractions, Lady Booby returns to the attack, only to be dumbfounded when her footman cites his 'virtue' as a prime ground for spurning her favours. She finds it quite incredible that any man can lay claim to such a quality, and matters are made much worse when Joseph earnestly cites his sister's good example. Lady Booby, who detests what she knows of that 'little vixen', can take no more of this, and when she sends for Slipslop (who has eavesdropped on the conversation anyway) to give poor Joseph the sack, is further angered by Slipslop's efforts to defend him and threatens to dismiss her too. Slipslop leaves in a huff, so Lady Booby orders her steward, Mr Peter Pounce, to deal with Joseph, but patches matters up with Slipslop who knows too much about Lady Booby to be safely turned off. Joseph is in the middle of another letter to Pamela when Peter Pounce sacks him, leaving him without clothes (the other servants, who like him, lend him some) and a few shillings from his pay, the rest having gone into Pounce's pocket as a part of an extortion racket amongst the servants by which the unscrupulous Pounce has made himself rich. As it is a moonlit night, Joseph sets off to walk home to Booby Hall.

Commentary
This is the real beginning of the novel's action. In his 'comic epic' Fielding has to follow the ancient Greek convention of opening epics *in medias res* (i.e. 'in the middle of things'). Accordingly we are plunged into the action and incidents follow thick and fast from the outset.

Lady Booby's shallow and selfish nature is pointed up by her total indifference to her husband's death and the bulk of this episode is concerned with the immediate siege she lays to Joseph's 'virtue' (a word Fielding deliberately works to death hereabouts in calculated parody of Richardson's unending reiteration of it in *Pamela*).

The episode is predominantly, though not entirely, humorous in its approach to the reader, but the humour ranges from such broadly comical effects as Fielding's treatment of Mrs Slipslop's 'allurements', rather in the style of a seaside comic postcard, to this sly dig at the end of his somewhat 'luscious' description of Joseph: '. . . an air which, to those who have not seen many noblemen, would give an idea of nobility'. This, at first suggests that Joseph compares poorly with the genuine article, but on reflection suggests that most 'noblemen' pale in comparison with him.

Fielding, in fact, operates his humorous devices at varying levels throughout. Because they will often recur, this may be a good occasion to identify some of them. First comes his sure hand with dramatic dialogue, a heritage from his career as a playwright. The scenes between Lady Booby and Slipslop are wickedly well-observed; they also make the point that the two women, for all the superficial differences in their speech, like Kipling's 'Colonel's lady and Judy O'Grady/Are sisters under the skin'.

The main comic strand, of course, is the way in which repeated waves of feminine passion are repelled by Joseph's implacable innocence. While we sympathise with poor Joseph we are of course bound to wonder whether anyone could possibly be quite so green as he is represented to be. And Fielding is, of course, using the inherent ludicrousness of the situation to mock at *Pamela* once more. Yet he is so poker-faced about this that we cannot be sure, and he may very well have been prompting his readers to take a closer look at their own prejudices when, after the splendidly elaborated account of Lady Booby's dumbstruck reaction to Joseph's pleading his 'virtue', he gives Joseph this simple rejoinder to her amazed disbelief. 'I can't see why [your] having no virtue should be a reason against my having any, or why, because I am a man, or because I am poor, my virtue should be subservient to [your] pleasures.' This has the ring of a very firmly held moral conviction, but we cannot say the same about Joseph's next artificial and pompous speech ending, ' . . . that boy is the brother of Pamela'. Unlike *Pamela* then, *Joseph* Andrews is not a simplistic book. Fielding can move from sardonic laughter to serious comment within a sentence or so.

Fieling makes use of mock 'epic' similes on four occasions in this episode. Such similes were employed seriously by Homer, Virgil and, in English, Milton (who e.g. compares Satan, in Book i of *Paradise Lost* with a whale so huge that seamen think it an island.) The idea is to lend 'immensity' and dignity to the object portrayed, whereas in mock epic the intention is the reverse, of course. This leads to Fielding's comparing Mrs Slipslop with 'a voracious pike' about to devour a 'roach or gudgeon', images as unflattering as they are low and vulgar. The same debunking trick is apparent in the address to Love at the end of Chapter 7 and in the simile for the conflict (in

Lady Booby) between Pity and Pride (Ch. 9). As with all burlesque this device relies, in part, on the reader's familiarity with the thing that is being guyed, and is, to that extent, not as funny to us as perhaps it was to some of Fielding's first readers. But we can still applaud the comic zest of the imagery.

The name Joseph which Fielding now substitutes for the diminutive Joey 'for a good reason' would in 1742 have immediately called to mind the biblical Joseph (Genesis, 37–50) who was a virtuous youth unjustly humiliated but later rising to greatness, and whose true identity was lost in his childhood owing to his abduction. The parallels are obvious enough and one may also notice that Fielding here gives the attentive reader more than a hint of a fortunate outcome for his hero. But the immediate point is that his biblical namesake, like Joseph Andrews, declined the favours offered him by the too-willing wife of Potiphar, his employer. Peter Pounce is an acrid little portrait, of a kind often to recur, in which Fielding goes some way beyond the good-humoured pillorying of 'affectation' towards acute, even vitriolic social criticism. Pounce was not untypical of many minor racketeers who exploited the generally illiterate lower servants of the day; the great houses with their armies of domestics offered rich opportunities for the unscrupulous to feather their nests. (*Note, pounce* was an eighteenth-century variant of *ponce*, with the same connotations as the latter word still has.)

Chapters 11–12. Summary

Fielding announces his intention to keep his readers guessing. He now reveals that Joseph's eagerness to return (to Lady Booby's country seat) is largely owing to his wish to see his childhood sweetheart Fanny Goodwill, who was also in the Boobys' employ-ment, until, jealous of her beauty, Mrs Slipslop dismissed her. She now works for a farmer and Joseph would have already married her had Adams not persuaded them to wait until their futures were more secure. They have only been able to exchange brief messages as Fanny cannot read or write, so that Joseph is on fire to see her again and walks at great speed. He luckily meets a former acquaintance who loans him his master's horse for twenty miles and tries, when they stop at an inn, to persuade him to borrow the horse again for the next day. But Joseph sets out again on foot, and is soon held up by two footpads. Although he gives them all his money, they demand he should strip so that they can have his clothes too, and, when he demurs, one strikes at him with a stick. Joseph parries the blow and knocks down his assailant but is in turn stunned by the other ruffian, stripped, beaten, as they suppose, to death, and left in the ditch. From this he is rescued, very reluctantly, and only because they fear to be held legally responsible for his death, by the occupants of a

passing stage-coach; the problem of his nakedness is only solved by
the willingness of the postilion – the poorest person present – to lend
him his own coat. Joseph's attackers now hold up the coach and rob
all the passengers, none of whom, though one has pistols, makes any
defence.

Various coarse jokes are made about Joseph's nakedness, en route
to their destination. When they arrive, only the good-natured serving
maid has pity on Joseph and puts him to bed. Next day her master,
Mr Tow-wouse, a weak but good-hearted man, offers Joseph a shirt,
but when his wife, the dragon-like Mrs Tow-wouse, discovers his
intention, she scarifies both Betty and him. While she is reading the
riot act to her husband, however, the local surgeon who has dressed
Joseph's wounds arrives with the news that Joseph is on the point of
death and so cannot be ejected.

Commentary
Fielding enjoys teasing his readers from time to time, as he does at
the start of Chapter 11. This is a luxury which those who rely upon
the appearance of authenticity, like Richardson, cannot afford
without giving the game away. Chapter 12 is fully analysed in the
Specimen Passage and Commentary.

Chapters 13–18. Summary
The surgeon returns to unload a good deal of medical jargon on
Joseph, whom he gloomily advises to make his will, but Joseph's only
thoughts are for Fanny. Accordingly, Mr Barnabas, the local vicar, is
sent for, and, after swallowing a few free drinks, he goes upstairs and
there overhears Joseph talking to himself in such an elevated style
that he supposes him to be delirious and beyond help. Later, he is
persuaded to return, and briskly absolves Joseph of his sins; not
without giving away his shaky knowledge of divinity.

Parson Adams (whose identity Fielding masks for a few pages)
arrives at the inn *en route* to London, and, sympathising with the – to
him anonymous – invalid upstairs, establishes, by questioning, the
surgeon's incompetence, at the price of suffering his feeble jests on
Adams's own learning. But when he recognises the bundle of clothes
which some young men have brought in as evidence against a thief
they have caught, he recognises them and is taken by Betty the
chambermaid to see Joseph. Betty has already returned Joseph a gold
piece (a love token from Fanny) also recovered from the thief, so
there is a happy reunion.

Attracted by the arrest of the thief a large company now assembles
at the inn, and airs some odd notions of the law. They persuade
themselves that there is no evidence against their prisoner, but, when

Betty cites the gold coin she has given Joseph, they change their minds and lock up the footpad for the night, since Joseph refuses to part with the coin, and isn't fit to appear as a witness.

On hearing from Betty that Adams, evidently a gentleman, is Joseph's friend, Mrs Tow-wouse, scenting a chance to make money, improves her arrangements at once. Adams tells Joseph that he is on his way to sell his sermons to a publisher in London, as he hopes, but will not desert his young friend. Moreover, he points out that Joseph's life is really in no danger, as all the surgeon wants is to have credit for his recovery. This welcome news cheers Joseph into eating a hearty meal. Barnabas and the surgeon (who are rivals in the amateur pursuit of the law) return to examine the prisoner who has, either by bribing or outwitting the constable, escaped. Adams, aware that his money is rapidly running out, attempts to borrow three guineas from Mr Tow-wouse, on the security of his sermons, but the landlord puts him off. A coach and six now arrives, and, after a noisy and vulgar exchange of boasts, bets and bad language, one of the newly arrived servants identifies Adams, whom Barnabas, up to then unaware he was a parson, now invites to share a bowl of punch with the surgeon. The two clergymen monopolise the talk with ecclesiastical gossip, Barnabas attempting to discourage Adams with tales of the multitude of sermons already in print.

Over the next three days Joseph recovers rapidly, and Adams resolves to let him go home alone, after all, while he will press on to London. At this point a bookseller friend of Barnabas's arrives, to Adams's delight, only for him to announce that sermons, unless by Methodists like Wesley or Whitefield, are a drug on the market. Mention of Whitefield enrages Barnabas, who thinks his literal interpretation of New Testament doctrine, and injunctions to poverty in particular, are heretical. Adams disputes this contention, and elaborates his own views, to the effect that Faith without Works is inadequate for salvation and apt to promote hypocrisy. His commendation of Hoadly's book on the sacrament and his contention that good heathens please God more than wicked Christians nearly produce apoplexy in Barnabas, who calls for the bill but is interrupted by a 'hideous uproar' occasioned by Mrs Tow-wouse's discovery of Betty in bed with her husband. Betty is given a piece of Mrs Tow-wouse's mind at full volume, together with the sack. She has, we learn, had previous misadventures of this kind, and, finding Joseph unresponsive to her charms has yielded to Mr Tow-wouse's persuasions, on the rebound.

Commentary

Fielding's extensive travels as a barrister on the Western Circuit had made him familiar with coaching inns, which were, in his time, centres for news, the post, and pretty well the only resort for company and conversation in nine-tenths of the country. The whole episode intermittently conveys a sharp flavour of the swirling, hectic movement which the continual arrival and departure of coaches and guests on horseback promoted. The major themes of the episode, which are intertwined, are first the exposure of a variety of affectations, illustrated in the portraits of the surgeon, Barnabas, and Mrs Tow-wouse especially, and secondly, pitted against these unpleasant and venal individuals, the portrait of Adams, here first fully treated, who stands for the positive qualities they pretend to but do not, as Fielding makes clear, possess.

Mrs Tow-wouse's is a brutal portrait, designed to show greed and self-regard at its most blatant. None the less the lady's about-turn from 'Common charity a fart' to 'God forbid she should not discharge the duty of a Christian,' when the conceives Joseph to be a gentleman with moneyed friends displays a common type of hypocrisy to perfection. The surgeon, who will not work without pay, is equipped with very little professional skill indeed. His medical terms, like his Latin and his Greek, are the merest gobbledegook (he locates Joseph's injuries at both the back and the top of his head and his 'radical small minute *invisible* nerve' is a phrase that Molière's *Mock Doctor* – a play Fielding translated – would have envied). These are, however, rather two-dimensional portraits, effective but limited in scope. Barnabas, as befits a fellow clergyman, is more fully and subtly handled in parallel with Adams. Aside from his fondness for free alcohol, his early conduct is not so reprehensible. He can hardly be blamed for supposing Joseph delirious, since his soliloquy is primarily a further dig at *Pamela* (who is addicted to recounting her own lengthy meditations in this fashion). Yet it is not a 'rhapsody of nonsense', ending as it does in a perfectly orthodox Christian reflection. But Barnabas as pastor begins to fall apart when his formal precepts: 'forget all carnal affections', etc. founder on the rock of Joseph's innocent honesty and simple piety. As between prayer and punch it is plain where his preference lies.

With the introduction, at first anonymously, of Adams to the scene (Ch. 14), the mockery of *Pamela* wanes rapidly and there soon follows a neat dissection of the motives of Barnabas and the surgeon in spending 'the whole night in debating' the case of the thief, a course of action neither would think of taking in pursuit of his proper profession. (The surgeon would not even get up to see Joseph on his arrival and Barnabas only attends him reluctantly next day.) This leads to Fielding's apostrophe to Vanity (the source of those Affectations which, as he said in Book I, Chapter 1, are his prime target). The high-flown style is derisory but the content is serious enough. Fielding did not wish to be thought pompous or pietistic in the manner that many of his predecessors in fiction had been, notably Richardson. But neither did he wish to be merely frivolous.

We now see proof that even the wise and kindly Adams is not entirely free from vanity, when he asserts to Tow-wouse that his sermons are 'as well worth a hundred pound as a shilling was worth twelve pence'. But his motive for pledging the sermons is wholly commendable. The uproar of a coach's arrival gives us Fielding in a reporter's guise. The railing and loose talk are precisely rendered, as with a tape-recorder, perhaps to point up the mixed company one may expect at an inn and to prepare the ground for a more 'serious' conversation about 'small tithes' and 'the hardships suffered by the minor clergy'. But the real object of the conversation is steadily to reveal Barnabas, who is superficially genial enough, in his true colours as a time-server. The conclusion, where Barnabas tries to cadge a sermon from Adams to use that day at a funeral, 'for which I have not penned a line, though I am to have a double price', is hilarious. Adams's subject, the strict and puritanical magistrate, is in perfect opposition to Barnabas's 'deceased upon whose virtues I am to harangue'. But Barnabas is sublimely unaware that anything like the truth is called for from the pulpit.

Fielding is far too shrewd to preach himself, and far too truthful to overplay Adams's hand. Indeed, he shows, by instancing '30th of January' sermons (which were notoriously vehicles for fierce political attacks, the date being that of Charles I's execution or martyrdom) that even the pulpit can pander to malice and uncharitableness, while Adams's eagerness to read a sample of his own work shows him not exempt from vanity. Yet Adams's measured reply to Barnabas's attack on Whitefield is a superb succinct rehearsal of the principles which Fielding sees as underpinning Christian life. The easy vigour of Adams's style, the sharp and even witty phrasing, for example 'Lord, it is true, I never obeyed one of thy commandments, yet punish me not, for I believe them all', the shocking – to the orthodox – ideas he puts forward (a 'good Turk' would have seemed a contradiction in terms to most people): all testify indirectly that Adams's sermons merit publication but will never get it. What Fielding is doing in this speech is setting up some touchstones for his readers to judge the actions of his characters – and perhaps their own too!

The bedroom farce which succeeds this may seem, and perhaps mostly is, intended to provide a farcical contrast to this seriousness. Even so we need to remind ourselves that Betty, though her 'generosity' is not perhaps in this case, to be commended, was, with the postilion, alone in acting charitably to the injured Joseph, and it may be that there is another biblical parallel here, with the woman taken in adultery of whom Jesus said, 'Let him who is without sin among you cast the first stone.' For Betty *is* kind, honest and warm-hearted, virtues Fielding thought went a long way to compensate for her other defects. Book I's concluding, long, beautifully controlled sentence (half a page of it) is masterly. No more perfect example of Fielding's acute, wry and witty perception of the human predicament is anywhere to be found than in the last few phrases.

Note. For anyone who wishes to pursue the biblical basis of Adams's and Barnabas's dispute over *Faith and Works*, the references are Matthew, vi, verses 19–24; xiii, verses 24–30; xix, verses 16–22; Mark, x, verses 23–25; St Paul's Epistle to the Romans, xiii, verses 13–14 (which is the key passage in what Adams says) and The Letter of James, ii, verses 14–26 (also of great importance).

Book ii

Chapter 1. Summary
Fielding discusses the various reasons for works being divided up into books and chapters, citing precedents from classical authors to support his own practice as well as revealing some of the 'tricks of the trade'.

Commentary
This is the second of the four more or less self-contained 'essays' which make up the opening chapters of each Book. It is of a kind, and written in a style, very familiar to eighteenth-century readers. The tone is typically ironic and self-deprecating throughout. 'Fine readers', it is mockingly implied, can only read a little at a time, chapter headings are an aid to skipping, the racket of part publication (still familiar today in magazine form) goes back to Homer, while the similes drawn from the tailor's bench and the butcher's block are designedly 'low', reducing literature to the status of a trade. While he is undoubtedly planting a few darts in the hide of authorial vanity and pedantry, Fielding is also simply enjoying himself, by 'sending up' pretentiousness – another form of 'affection'.

Chapters 2–3. Summary
As they are about to go their several ways, Joseph discovers that Adams has forgotten to bring his sermons. Adams, unperturbed, decides to return with Joseph, pays the bill out of a guinea he has borrowed from a former parishioner, and sets off, leaving Joseph to follow on the horse as the first stage of the 'ride and tie' system, which Fielding explains. But Adams has omitted to pay the bill for the horse's fodder, and, though she might otherwise have let him owe the money, when the covetous Mrs Tow-wouse catches sight of Joseph's gold keepsake she demands it, and refuses to release the horse albeit he will not be parted from it.

Adams, who has soaked himself by unnecessarily wading through a pond, and is worried by Joseph's failure to catch him up, learns of his protegé's predicament at an inn, where he overhears two newly arrived lawyers discussing its legal aspects. In conversation with these travellers Adams hears, first that a local landowner is a monster of iniquity, and then – from the other lawyer in the absence of the first – that he is notably virtuous and benevolent. When they have left, the perplexed Adams seeks enlightenment from the landlord and is disgusted to learn that their contradictory accounts are both tissues of falsehood, arising from the common factor that the landowner, a Justice of the Peace, gave a decision in favour of one and against the other. His condemnation of lying evokes little agreement from the landlord who proves to be a churchgoer on whom his religion bears so lightly as to be unnoticeable.

A coach arrives bearing Mrs Slipslop on her way to Booby Hall, and followed shortly by Joseph, whose horse Mrs Slipslop, who retains a fancy for him, has redeemed. Adams accepts a lift in it, Joseph rides after, and, following some malicious disclosures about Lady Booby from Slipslop, another passenger undertakes to tell the story of a lady who lives nearby.

Commentary

Not much need be said of Chapter 2, which is largely concerned to advance the narrative, though a final acid touch is added to the abominable Mrs Tow-wouse and Adams's unworldly behaviour is once more instanced. Chapter 3 brings in the law. Fielding is no more gently disposed towards his own profession than to others, and here he dextrously presents advocates who, paid to present a one-sided case, carry the habit into their private lives and become indifferent to the truth. Indeed the nature of truth is what the chapter is really about; the landlord is a sketch of the easy-going conformist who has no real convictions, while Mrs Slipslop is quite prepared to reverse her opinions at the drop of a hat. Adams's own profound concern is demonstrated by his scrupulous qualification of his own truthfulness. He will not assert that he has 'never' told a lie, only that he has never told a malicious or injurious one. In this way Fielding avoids making him too good to be true.

Chapters 4–6. Summary

Note. Because Chapters 4 and 6 tell a continuous story (with 5 as comic relief) I shall summarise and comment on *The History of Leonora* first.

Leonora who is a lively, pretty, but vain and rather shallow girl, accepts, not without coquetry, the proposal of Horatio, a decent young man who is beginning to make his way as a lawyer but is far from wealthy. The wedding is only two weeks off when, in Horatio's absence, she attends a ball. Here she encounters a handsome stranger from France, named Bellarmine, whose looks, dress, manners and conversation are so ostentatiously fashionable and extravagant that she is both flattered and attracted when he asks her to dance. She loses her heart and her rather empty head to him, albeit he, we learn, has a weather eye on her father's money. Egged on by her coldly

unscrupulous and calculating aunt, she rationalises her impulsive
decision to jilt Horatio. She is entertaining Bellarmine when Horatio
unexpectedly returns to confront them. She speaks to her fiancé in
tones of fleering contempt, a quarrel ensues, though not of his
making, and her aunt enters in time to prevent Horatio taking his
horse-whip to Bellarmine. But contrary to the aunt's contemptuous
prediction, Horatio not only challenges Bellarmine but also runs him
through. He iş reported to be dying, and now the aunt ruthlessly
advises Leonora to drop him and try to recover Horatio's affections.
At this Leonora furiously puts all the blame for her misfortunes on
her aunt's counsel, and, when a letter from Bellarmine arrives with
news that he is not dangerously ill, she rushes off to become his
nurse, indifferent to the scandal this creates. When, however, a
restored Bellarmine visits her father to press his suit, that miserly old
curmudgeon, whilst accepting the proposal, flatly declines to give his
daughter the dowry without which Bellarmine will on no account
marry her. He leaves for Paris, writing Leonora one dismissive letter,
which leaves her, with her reputation ruined, plunged into despon-
dency, to live out her life as a recluse and never see Horatio again,
though he has never forgotten her.

Commentary
Fielding is perhaps making some concession to his readers' tastes with
this predictable, and rather heavy-handed, cautionary tale, since such
self-contained moral anecdotes were a staple of earlier fiction.
Nevertheless, the tale does bear upon the larger narrative. Its major
themes are varieties of vanity and affectation, it continues Fielding's
assault upon the corrupting influence of wealth and fashion, while the
aunt – a venomous little cameo – with her shallow precepts for
'success', is to be seen as a contrast with Adams, whose advice, if not
always practicable, is never materialistic.

Chapter 5. Summary
The coach stops at an inn, where Adams finds Joseph in the kitchen,
having his leg treated for injuries sustained while riding Adams's
ill-trained horse. The inn-keeper angrily objects to his wife's kindly
attentions, and attempts to eject Joseph, whereupon Adams lays him
out, has a large pan of hogsblood thrown over him by the inn-
keeper's wife, and is promptly avenged by Slipslop who sets about the
landlady with relish. The outcry attracts the other travellers, and
peace is restored, at which first the inn-keeper and then Adams are,
unsuccessfully, advised by 'gentlemen' (probably lawyers) to press
charges of assault against each other. Back in the coach, Mrs Slipslop
vehemently abuses Miss Grave-airs, a prudish passenger, for object-
ing to Joseph's sharing the compartment, only to be disconcerted by
the arrival of Miss Grave-airs's father, a very wealthy self-made man,

in whose coach she departs, leaving the other ladies to dissect her character energetically.

Commentary

The immediate objective of this interlude is to provide some light relief but it is rather more cleverly interwoven with the *Leonora* tale than appears at first glance. Though farcical indeed the scene would work splendidly on stage – it is not merely knockabout. Thus the inn-keeper, whose relationship with his wife is a deliberate inversion of the Tow-wouses' feud, is a further exemplification of uncharitableness, the bloody combat is a ludicrous parallel with the Horatio–Bellarmine duel, the absurd 'gentleman from Italy' carries the affectations of Bellarmine a stage further and Slipslop's self-seeking is on a par with the aunt's. The whole business, set in a kitchen, acted out among ordinary people, deflates by its absurdity the combats which formed so large a part of fashionable romances, an inversion very much in the manner of *Don Quixote*. The 'elevated' language which Fielding employs to describe the brawl – 'so sound a compliment', 'assailed his antagonist', 'saluted his countenance' — is mock-heroic, directed at the false sentiments and rodomontade of Leonora and Bellarmine. And, for all its roughness, the world of the country inn is also plainly to be preferred to that of the fashionable town.

Chapters 7–11

Adams, inevitably, forgets his horse, and, imagining the coach which follows him to be challenging him to a race, out-distances it and then contrives to lose himself thoroughly. By chance he finds a sportsman out after partridge who soon proves himself to be, at least in word, a valiant patriot who would readily die for his country. By way of showing what *he* has done for his country, Adams relates a part of his life-story. It emerges that, though he was lucky enough to have, as nephew, an Alderman with great political influence, Adams, too scrupulous to use it for his own advancement in the Church, has rather tried to promote the interests of the Church at elections which his nephew has been in a position to control. These efforts, owing to the venality of those elected, have neither benefited the Church nor Adams, who, with his nephew now dead, cannot even promote his son's ordination.

In reply, the sportsman confides that he has himself disinherited a nephew for cowardice, and maintains that all cowards should be hanged, which Adams thinks too severe. As the 'man of courage' is reiterating his views they hear a scream, at which Adams attempts to grab the gun and – though it is now pitch-dark – sally to the rescue. He is staggered to see his fire-eating companion make a run for it, clutching the gun in his 'trembling' hand. Undaunted, he makes for the source of the scream and, finding a man assaulting a woman, strikes the would-be rapist with his cudgel. After a protracted battle,

Adams stuns his opponent but the woman is still frightened and suspicious, while he is concerned that he may have killed the rapist, so both are initially pleased at the arrival of a party of bird-baiters. Their account of what happened is interrupted by the ingenious villain who, plausibly enough, contends that Adams and his victim have really set upon and tried to rob *him*. In the event all three are hauled off to appear before the local magistrate. On the way Adams and Fanny, who having heard of Joseph's injury had set off immediately to find him, recognise each others' voices.

The court is held in the local JP's dining-room. He has added a generous measure of alcohol to his natural stupidity, and without waiting to hear the evidence, decides on Adams and Fanny as the guilty parties. A disgraceful parody of court procedure ensues, with much baiting of Adams and a general display of ignorance and prejudice. However, as the magistrate is on the point of committing Adams and Fanny to the assizes for trial, Squire Booby (now presumably Pamela's husband) recognises Adams, and upon his informing the JP that Adams is a clergyman and thus also a gentleman the magistrate immediately releases him and Fanny, only to find the real villain has sneaked off. Adams accepts the offer of refreshment from the magistrate, and a violent brawl breaks out next door between the bird watchers who are in angry disagreement as to how much reward they *would* have received if they had caught a criminal. Adams and Fanny accept the offer of a guide to the place where Joseph is staying.

Commentary
This episode is primarily concerned with the dissection of three varieties of affectation hitherto only lightly touched on. First is the issue of political cant, second the coward's pretence to courage, and finally ignorance masquerading as learning. All three are viewed in their relationship with Adams, who is, as usual, the touchstone of right conduct; the second and last are both interwoven with the miscarriage of justice, which so nearly dooms Adams and Fanny to gaol in Chapter 7.

Adams, as is his invariable custom, believes implicitly what the 'man of courage' asserts, though Fielding gives his readers a strong hint, by way of the sportsman's extravagant phrasing, that we should take all these protestations with a large pinch of salt. Self-sacrifice having been mentioned, Adams, always a willing conversationalist, sets forth a sad account of his failure to make use of the 'interest' he once had with his nephew the Alderman, to his own advantage. Here we need to remind ourselves that the form of nepotism referred to was – though theoretically barred of course – so much the most common, indeed often the *only* way to obtain any advancement in the eighteenth century, that even the scrupulous Adams does not demur at its employment. Through Adams Fielding raises a thorny question;

can true Christianity co-exist with a modicum of cynicism? If Adams is our exemplar, the answer is 'No'; but are we all really required to be as ingenuous as he is? Adams's trusting naivety here, therefore, spotlights the yawning gulf between things as they are and as they ought to be, where the welfare of the commonwealth is at issue.

We now know Fielding's methods well enough to anticipate the arrant poltroonery of Adams's new acquaintance. Nevertheless, his fluent attempt to justify himself in Chapter 9 is a beautifully malicious example of Fielding's genius for catching mankind with its talent for rationalising its inadequacies in full flow: 'Do you consider this gun is *only charged with shot*, and that the robbers are most probably furnished with pistols *loaded with bullets*. This is no business of *ours* . . .' [My italics]. Such ingenuities, in other contexts, are not unknown to most of us. It is a sharp piece of psychological insight that has Fanny still in fear of her unrecognisable 'deliverer' who, in a typical romance, she would indubitably have bedewed with tears of gratitude. Fielding has a very well-developed sense of how people really behave in situations fraught with stress.

We now come to the court scene, a superb set-piece. Few men have had a higher respect for the law than Fielding. As a Justice in London he was exceptional in his total incorruptibility, in his determination to protect the weak, the poor and the innocent from exploitation and brutality. Accordingly he hated the abuse and distortion of justice vehemently, and in this scene corruscatingly displays ignorance, malice, prejudice and bullying in action. The general tenor of what happens is plain enough not to need any comment, of course. However, it may be worth while picking out how nearly every precedent and custom of the common law is flouted. It is only with difficulty that the clerk persuades the JP to take statements at all (i.e. *depositions*), as he is anxious to decide the issue without even hearing the case. His attitude makes a mockery of the precept that the accused is 'innocent until proved guilty' while it is plain that he has never heard of a 'reasonable doubt' and wouldn't, in his drunken state, recognise one if it bit him. He pays no attention at all, contrary to his sworn oath as a magistrate, to 'hear' both sides, to investigate the charges, albeit even a moment's consideration would have shown that one party *must* be lying and that questioning is therefore called for. The whole 'Aeschylus' business plumbs depths of absurdity, no doubt, but it is also a fierce indictment of ignorance and prejudice in action. And if perhaps the JP is a caricature, as he is certainly not meant to be typical of his kind, yet Fielding now touches upon a grave and widespread abuse. For when Adams cries: 'Is it no punishment, sir, for an innocent man to lie several months in gaol?' he is voicing an all-too-prevalent complaint. Assizes were infrequent, bail, except for the rich and influential, unobtainable, and gaol not only deprived a man of his freedom but as often as not killed him by the endemic and incurable gaol fever before he ever came to trial. For all the jests, mostly bitter in flavour, this is an intensely serious passage, a powerful plea for the improvement of an institution unique to England, the lay magistracy.

Chapter 12– 17. Summary

Adams and Fanny have accepted the services of a guide to Joseph's inn, but a downpour prompts them to stop at the first they reach. Fielding chooses this moment to describe Fanny's, somewhat voluptuous, charms. She recognises Joseph's voice, singing next door, and the lovers, to their rapturous delight – though not to Mrs Slipslop's who is also present – are re-united. Mrs Slipslop affects to have totally forgotten Fanny, who worked with her for years at Booby Hall, which is the occasion for Fielding to interpose a reflection upon 'high and low people', or, as we should say on social standing, and on 'fashion'. Mrs Slipslop is on the point of quarrelling with Adams, whose rescue of Fanny she regards as conduct unbefitting a clergy-man, when the coach's departure is announced. Having failed in her attempt to persuade Joseph (whom she hoped to have to herself at the inn) to abandon Fanny and accompany her, she leaves, in high dudgeon.

The happy Joseph now proposes marriage to Fanny, who accepts, but Adams naturally will not marry them on the spot. Next day, presented with the bill, they cannot pay. Adams visits the local incumbent, the gross and bestial Parson Trulliber, who much res-embles the pigs which are his true avocation. Supposing Adams to be a pig dealer, he urges him into a sty where Adams slips and covers himself with muck. When Adams has explained who he really is, Trulliber's behaviour marginally softens, until Adams requests a loan. Flabbergasted, Trulliber, who is as miserly as he is greedy, quotes a parable which Adams mistakenly supposes to be evidence of sympathy, but Trulliber's ensuing fury disabuses him. Adams, sharply pointing out that Trulliber's conduct is inconsistent with the gospel he preaches, leaves his hat and coat behind in his haste to be off. When the landlady fetches them she hears from Trulliber that her guests are penniless and detains them until her bill can be paid. By good fortune a travelling pedlar lends them all he has, which is just enough to settle the bill, together with Adams's last sixpence.

At their next halt they meet an engaging gentleman, who offers them drinks, strongly condemns the conduct of the local parson (presumably Trulliber) and apparently takes so strong a liking to Adams that he there and then offers him the reversion of a living in his 'gift' (i.e. a parish to which he can appoint the vicar), of which he says the holder is very old and infirm. He also invites them to stay with him and extends the loan of his coach for the next day. When they accept he makes excuses. His house is, he says, not fit for occupation so that they remain at the inn, only to find, next day, that no coach arrives either. The landlord then reveals that all the gentleman's promises, including the living, are false. Adams, more so than Joseph who has seen this kind of behaviour in London, is amazed and horrified at such apparently motiveless malignancy, but the landlord's cheerful readiness to extend credit, even on such poor security as they can offer, restores his always sanguine faith in humanity. Fanny and Joseph sit in the garden while the landlord gives more, and worse, examples of the lying squire's worthless promises, of which he himself, when young, was a victim. Upon Adams saying that the squire's face shows good-nature, the landlord, who as a sailor has travelled widely, says that appearances count for nothing. They then fall into a dispute about the relative merits of experience and authority, which leads them on to argue bad-temperedly about the usefulness to mankind of trade versus learning. But the return of Joseph and Fanny breaks off the dispute, and the three set off again.

Commentary

It is difficult to generalise about this episode, which is something of a rag-bag, rather tenuously held together by its location at an inn. In so far as there is a unifying thread it is succinctly expressed by Fielding's acute – and two-edged – remark about Adams as knowing no more of the everyday world than 'the cat which [sits] on the table'. If ever Adams were to have acquired a modicum of scepticism about the motives of his fellow mortals he surely ought, one feels, to have done so by the end of Book II.

Thus, Fielding's acrid dissection of the differences between 'high' and 'low' people, in which his chief intention is to point up the essential triviality of the social ladder on whose rungs position is decreed by 'fashion', is instantly reinforced by Adams's entirely innocent and ' benevolent insistence that Mrs Slipslop should acknowledge Fanny.

It is important to realise that Trulliber, who appears to us an almost absurd caricature in his greed, ignorance, and coarseness, would have been, to Fielding's contemporaries, a recognisable, if exaggerated, type. He is plainly ill-educated, quite unfitted to be the spiritual mentor of his parishioners, though he might have been able to give them points on pig-breeding, but his initial behaviour to Adams is not malicious of intent. Here, Fielding is making the point that many of the rural clergy, paid only a pittance in cash, were forced to resort to their 'glebe' (i.e. their holding of land) for subsistence; to become, in effect, small farmers. This is no excuse, of course, for Trulliber's reaction to Adams's proposal that he should, by lending him seven shillings, take an 'opportunity of laying up treasure in a better place than this world affords.' Adams's reference to the *Sermon on the Mount* (Matthew VI, verses 19–21) would not have been lost even upon a man so steeped in ignorance as Trulliber. When finally disabused of his notions of Trulliber's charity, Adams is more severe and condemnatory than he is to anyone else. Fielding here returns to his constant stress on the necessity of good works to the Christian, but Adams's stern pronouncement, which is phrased so that it could easily be biblical, 'whoever, therefore, is void of charity, I make no scruple of pronouncing that he is no Christian' sounds, and is meant to sound, literally damning.

The finishing touch is given by the poor pedlar's readiness to lend all he has, another incident which has biblical overtones (Mark XII, verses 41–44), being an echo of the parable of the widow's mite.

Chapter 17 is linked to its predecessors in so far as both illustrate the painful difference between appearance and reality. But whereas only Adams's essential goodness would mistake Trulliber's real nature for long, anyone might be (indeed, as it turns out, many have been) deceived by the 'courteous and obliging gentleman' whom the travellers meet at their next stop. He is a polished hypocrite, saying all the right things and quick-witted enough to retreat from extending his criticism of Trulliber to a general indictment of the clergy when he sees this offends Adams. Though Joseph, out of his disillusioning London sojourn, has grounds for suspicion, he keeps them to himself, and Adams is a long time accepting that his benefactor is, in fact, a 'monster'. There is indeed something inhuman and satanic about his sadistic enjoyment of deceit and its consequent painful realisation. Up to this point, Fielding's characters, however reprehensible, have had some recognisable motive for their malice, lust, greed, avarice, and pride. Now we have hate, masquerading as love, for humanity and doing 'the devil's work for nothing' as Adams puts it. But the man obviously enjoys his own malevolent deceptions and this makes the landlord's subsequent benevolence the more effective as a contrast.

The last chapter picks up a dispute which is certainly as old as written literature, probably much older. What exercises Adams and the landlord, albeit they use the terms 'trade' and 'learning' is really the conflict – or apparent conflict between 'experience' and 'authority'. Fielding creates a spirited and even-handed debate, which arises out of Adams's pedantic insistence, vexing to the reader let alone the landlord, that in spite of all his own experience to the contrary, one can read a man's nature in his face. This, as it affects the chameleon-like squire, is so obviously absurd, as the landlord himself has the best reason for knowing, that it is not in the least odd to find him rejecting it. Yet what he asserts about the prime importance of 'trade' is equally open to objections, of course. It is an entertaining diversion certainly, but whether it is of much relevance to the book as a whole is open to question.

Book III

Chapter 1. Summary

Biography (by which Fielding must in what follows be understood to mean the novel) is generally superior to History, so-called, because, however scrupulously historians may assemble their factual materials, it is clear that differences in viewpoint and presentation will produce such vast gaps between one historian's work and another's that they might as well have invented them. This is particularly true of their handling of men's characters, where the same person may be seen as a rogue and a hero, according to which viewpoint the historian takes up.

The reverse is true of biographers (i.e. novelists of Fielding's kind), in that they are primarily concerned to display universal truths about human nature and minor factual details, if incorrect, are of no real significance to them. Fielding excludes from this commendation, however, those 'modern novelists and Atlantis writers' whose books are mere fantasies, instancing *Don Quixote* as 'the history of the world in general', by which he means that it is of universal and continual relevance to the human predicament in the civilised world, at least.

His own creations in *Joseph Andrews*, for example the lawyer (Book I, Ch. 12) and Mrs Tow-wouse (Book I, Ch. 12–17) represent, he claims, 'not men, but manners; not an individual, but a species', yet they are nevertheless immediately recognisable as authentic and life-like portraits, satiric and corrective (as opposed to libellous) attacks upon vice rather than on vicious individuals. In conclusion, he warns his readers that his critical generalisations about whole classes of society (e.g. 'high people') are not really intended to apply to all members of a particular class, but only to the minority who are a discredit to it.

Commentary

This introductory chapter, strategically placed half-way through the book, is partly a restatement of the objectives announced in the *Author's Preface* and partly an explanation and defence of his own practice as a writer. Fielding's comments on 'history' are perhaps only half-serious; his indictment of historians' inability to agree is nevertheless telling. What follows, though it bears witness to Fielding's unusually wide reading of fiction, would need lengthy notes to elucidate in detail. The central point is Fielding's care to discriminate between good novelists like Le Sage (author of *Gil Blas*, 1715) and Scarron (author of *Le Roman Comique*, 1651) and other 'writers of surprising genius' – 'surprising' is a typically two-edged Fielding epithet – whom he goes on to praise, with withering irony, for having severed all contact with reality.

His admiration for Cervantes is unbounded if perhaps also liable to misinterpretation. When Fielding says that *Don Quixote* is a 'history of the world in general' we need to remember that the word *history* was then used in a much looser and less technical sense than it is today. We might then paraphrase his comment as 'a book exhibiting those aspects of human behaviour which do not change from place to place or from time to time'. This, naturally, leads to his defence of his own method in the next paragraph, where, following classical precedent, he argues that it is better to present a 'species' than an 'individual'. This, speaking generally, is what he does (though if we go back to the Author's Preface we shall see that he acknowledges an exception in Adams). But before we dismiss his creations as mere 'types' we must consider that many of them have very restricted functions in the book; the lawyer and Mrs Tow-wouse, for example, are there to do exactly what Fielding says, 'to hold the glass to thousands'. We may feel that he had no need to assure his audience that his generalisations about members of a given social class ('high people') do not apply to every member of that class. But this is a timely reminder, for us, that Fielding's concept of the novel was new, and that his audience was totally unfamiliar with such work.

Chapters 2–4. Summary
Note. Although Chapter 2 is self-contained it owes its existence simply to the need to bring about a meeting between Wilson and the travellers, so forming a lead-in to Mr Wilson's story of his life.

Adams, Fanny and Joseph are benighted and taking a rest when they see weird lights and hear, apparently murderous, voices and blows. Uncertain whether these are human or ghostly, they run away, and after Adams has precipitately tumbled and rolled down a hill they ask for shelter at a house and are made welcome. Here they shortly learn that the cause of their retreat was neither ghosts nor murderers but sheep-stealers whom their host's shepherds have caught. By way of testing Adams's claim to be a clergyman, which his appearance makes dubious, their host institutes a conversation about literature, which gives Adams the opportunity for a lengthy and enthusiastic discourse on Homer, whose *Iliad* he prefers to his *Odyssey*, and whose works he rates more highly than those of the other Greeks, even his favourite Aeschylus. Their host, much impressed, invites all three to bed and board, and after they have had supper and the ladies have retired, he first requests Joseph's story and then, in return agrees to Adams's suggestion that he should relate his own autobiography.

Note. As the details of Wilson's story, Fielding's second major digression, are not really germane to the narrative of *Joseph Andrews* as a whole, what follows is drastically condensed.

After Wilson has, aged only sixteen, inherited a substantial fortune, he takes the advice of his lawyers to contest, with the trustees, his father's intention that he should not receive the inheritance until he is twenty-five. He leaves school and goes to London where he speedily learns to act the part of a man about town, becoming fashionably cynical, foul-mouthed, and also – in reality – idle and bored. He is challenged to a duel but backs out, frightened, and retreats to live at the Temple where he forms new, and even worse friendships, and, resorting to brothels, contracts venereal disease. Once cured, he first keeps a mistress, and then debauches a beautiful, but impoverished, young girl, who ultimately leaves him, becomes a prostitute, and dies in prison. His intrigue with a married woman results in a prosecution and he attempts to recoup the money he has lost by it in play-writing, which however, does not compensate him for his gambling losses. Reduced to cadging from the wealthy and making small sums by working as a hack writer, he is arrested for debt. He is, however, released from prison through the generosity of the daughter of the man to whom Wilson had, as a last resort, sold his lottery ticket, a winning one as it turned out. Her father having died suddenly, she sends Wilson £200, with which he settles his debts. He has secretly admired her for some time, and when she accepts his proposal of marriage, they retire to live on a small estate in the country. Their simple way of life and delight in their own self-sufficiency is marred only by the disappearance of their only son, stolen by gipsies from his cradle.

Next day, the whole company, and especially Mr Wilson's three young daughters are much upset by the local squire's wanton shooting of their pet dog. This incident upsets their happy stay and the travellers set out again.

Commentary
Little need be said about Chapter 2; the mishaps by night are both an overture to, and a calculated contrast with, the pause for rest and refreshment at Mr Wilson's house. There is nothing particularly improbable about either the events (sheep stealing was widespread, sometimes incurring the death penalty) or the fear of the supernatural. Even the great Dr Samuel Johnson believed in the possibility of ghosts and it was generally a superstitious age.

Mr Wilson's story is a good deal more than padding. As a follow-up to Joseph's account of his life (which Fielding obviously has no need to summarise here) it shows us the other side of the coin; what happens when a young man who has all the advantages Joseph lacks; wealth, education, good family, etc. sets out on a course of action which Oscar Wilde summed up as 'Always yield to temptation'. The point of this brutally frank account is the emptiness, the ultimate self-disgust, which, more than any condign punishment, can be expected as the consequence of a life without principles of any kind. If one were disposed to think that Fielding was really indifferent to chastity, that Joseph was to be laughed at for not taking his opportunity, the sombre and pitiable fate of Wilson's mistresses should clear that misconception up, as should his thrice repeated 'visit to the surgeon'.

Adams's reactions are what principally sustain our interest and there is one particularly neat touch when, just as Wilson reaches the climax of his bitter harangue on vanity as the worst of passions, Adams breaks in to lament bitterly that he has not got his 'masterpiece', a sermon on vanity, with him. His readiness to go ten miles to fetch it, undiscouraged by Wilson's polite indifference, is maliciously set beside his firm avowal that he has ' . . . never been a greater enemy to any passion than that silly one of vanity'. By such small touches as this, Fielding continually reminds us that Adams is, however good, never inhumanly so.

Chapter 5. *Summary*
Joseph and Adams fall to discussing schools and schooling as they walk, and Adams attributes much of Wilson's ill-spent and profligate youth to his having been at a 'public' (i.e. a boarding) school, as distinct from a 'private' one (such as were run, to augment their incomes, by many country clergymen, the pupils lodging in their homes, a system which it would seem, Adams himself has at one time time employed). Adams thinks the public schools are 'nurseries of vice and immorality', but Joseph adduces the argument of his former master, the late Sir Thomas Booby, that, since 'great' (i.e. large) public schools are images of society at large, they prepare their pupils for the world as it is, a point Adams thinks, makes them worse, not better, inasmuch as 'private schools', he says, protect a boy's innocence and preserve him from temptation. Joseph disagrees, arguing from his own experience that a wickedly disposed person will follow his proclivities, irrespective of his school, whereas the firmer discipline of public schools will at least keep such persons under control. Adams, whose one real weakness is his extremely high opinion of his own teaching abilities, is on the verge of losing his temper when, having reached a particularly lovely and secluded spot, they agree to stop for their lunch.

Commentary
This is not as much a digression as it seems, displaying as it does, not only that no man is without his vanities, but that Joseph's native intelligence can enable him to keep his end up. But the passage doesn't just put the pros and cons of two differing types of education; it also rehearses the arguments for two moral and religious viewpoints, since Adams is really contending for what we should call environment and Joseph for heredity in this dispute, whereas, from the religious viewpoint Joseph contends for predestination and Adams for free-will. Fielding's brief description of the glade is

interesting in its employment of the adjective 'romantic' in an
unusually 'modern' sense, as well as for its evidential value as to
Fielding's eye for natural beauty.

Chapters 6–7. Summary

Joseph, at some length, discourses to Fanny and a somnolent Adams
on the value of charity in action, pointing out that whereas expensive
possessions reflect credit on their creators rather than their
purchasers, acts of generosity, instead of causing envy, create respect
and admiration, as well as being intrinsically good. Charity is the
high-road to a deserved good name. Seeing that Adams has fallen
asleep, Joseph draws Fanny aside for a little 'dalliance'.

The local hunt, in hot pursuit of a hare, now arrives. The hounds
make their kill next to Adams, and they then begin to worry his
cassock as he lies asleep. This awakens him and he takes to his heels,
hotly pursued by the pack, urged on by the squire. Joseph hastens to
the rescue and he and Adams fight off the dogs with their cudgels
until the huntsman calls them off. The enraged master and his friends
are distracted by Fanny's beauty, and somewhat mollified to find only
two hounds killed. The squire therefore, by way of apology, though
also with an ulterior motive, invites all three travellers to his house,
and Adams to dinner that evening. The squire, a wealthy, self-
indulgent bachelor, besides his addiction to hunting and the bottle,
has an obsession with the grotesque, and has acquired a group of
toadying hangers-on, each of whom is in some way odd. At dinner a
variety of crude practical jokes is played on the unsuspecting Adams,
until – a squib having been tied to his cassock – even he realises what
is going on, and sternly rebukes his host and his henchmen, in a
dignified speech. Pretending to be ashamed, they inveigle him into
delivering a sermon from a trick throne, which precipitates him into a
tub of water, into which however, he succeeds in dragging the squire
too. Pausing only to collect Joseph and Fanny, he leaves the house.

Commentary

Joseph's disquisition on charity (yet another return to this dominant
motif in the novel) is also, of course, a tribute to his sterling good
sense. The speech is also part of the process (begun in Chapter 17 of
Book II) of filling out, one might say 'solidifying', Joseph's character,
from the rather shadowy outline, almost entirely physical, given at
the outset of the action. As a conclusion to these, rather static,
scenes, we are also given a glimpse into Fanny's gentler nature, when
the hare is killed. Fielding, with one of his abrupt changes of pace and
mood, now thrusts us into a sequence of exuberant knockabout, with,
however, more menacing undertones. He embellishes the battle with
a sustained flight of mock heroics, in which absurd (but recognisable)
contemporary scenes and characters are substituted in the description
of the decoration of Joseph's cudgel, for those depicted (in Homer's

Iliad) on the shield of Achilles – a famous passage known, at least in translation, to anyone with claims to wide reading at that time. Regrettably, few things wear less well than burlesque, and to us, unfamiliar with the pomposities of the works Fielding is guying here, a little goes a long way.

In Chapter 7 Fielding slyly begins with an example of just that kind of private education that Adams has been extolling to Joseph, in the unpleasant person of the squire. Wealthy, self-indulgent, dissolute, addicted to flattery, he is quite devoid of 'the plain spirit and honesty of our ancestors' – a phrase which tells us a good deal about Fielding's views on some of his contemporaries. The squire's obsession with the grotesque and perverse is all of a piece with the 'roasting' of Adams. His delight in ridiculing 'virtue and wisdom' makes him the antithesis of such men as Ralph Allen of Bath, whom Fielding admired and twice refers to (III, 1 'I could name a commoner . . .' and III, 6, Joseph speaking of 'another at the Bath, one Al-, Al- . . .').

In general the episode demonstrates that all attempts to degrade by ridicule genuine (as opposed to hypocritical) virtue are ineffectual. If the idea was to expose Adams as not practising the virtues he professes, his calm but magisterial rebuke to the sycophantic company, and his ready, warm, forgiveness, are a sufficient answer. The squire degrades his position in society by insulting a guest, the 'gentlemen' around his table are far more cruel and childish in their pastimes than are their social 'inferiors'.

Chapters 8–13. Summary
Note. These six chapters, although they include one acknowledged digression (Chapter 10) constitute a single episode in so far as the narrative is concerned.

Adams, who has collected Joseph and Fanny from the kitchens, leads them away from the squire's house. The darkness enables them to evade pursuit and they find their way to the New Inn, seven miles off. Here, dining off bread, cheese and beer, Adams falls into conversation with a Roman Catholic priest. The priest is travelling incognito, for if his identity had been disclosed he would have been liable to an enormous fine or prison; to celebrate Mass was technically treason. He and Adams enthusiastically join in a general condemnation of money, which, they agree, can purchase nothing of true value. Regrettably from his and the priest's point of view (who now begins to suspect Adams's motives) it is at this point that Adams has to refuse a loan of eighteen pence, because he has had his pocket picked at the squire's dinner. The landlord reluctantly gives the priest credit and is subsequently rebuked by Adams for exhibiting regret at his decision to be charitable.

In Chapter 9 the inn is invaded by the squire's henchmen, who, after a violent battle in which Joseph fells the captain with a stone chamber-pot, overpower her two defenders and abduct Fanny, intending to deliver her to the squire who hopes to seduce, or perhaps to rape her. Joseph and Adams are left, tied to the bedposts, the innkeeper having been brow-beaten into compliance with the squire's wishes. Meanwhile the poet and the player (i.e. playwright and actor, as we should say) dodge the battle upstairs and discuss their vocations. They begin with mutual flattery and fulsome compliment, but the poet is piqued by the player's inability to recall a 'tender speech' in the third act of his play, and immediately they fall to recrimination and angry abuse, each blaming the other for the play's failure on the stage. In Chapter 11 the pinioned Adams attempts to allay Joseph's passionate and helpless grief for his lost Fanny, by putting forward sound theological arguments why he should submit to, and even benefit from his misfortunes. Of these, Adams says, he can neither know the cause nor the outcome, except that they are expressions of the Divine will. His best efforts, however, only pour salt into the wound.

In Chapter 12 we return to Fanny whom the captain is forcibly conveying to the squire's home. He makes plain the squire's evil intentions, threatening her with violence if she attempts to escape. However, she appeals to two passing horsemen, who prove to be Lady Booby's servants, one of whom recognises her, and takes her part. They are armed, and when Peter Pounce, whose coach they are escorting to Booby Hall, arrives in it, his susceptibility to a pretty face prompts him to have the captain arrested, tied up and brought along behind the coach, in which Fanny accepts a lift. Once back at the New Inn, Fanny rushes to free her companions. Peter, basking in Adams's sincere, if misplaced, admiration, orders the captain to be brought before him, preparatory to committing him to appear before the magistrates, but learns that Joseph has already interviewed him with a cudgel for his behaviour to Fanny, and the servants, who thought the thrashing sufficient, have let him go. After a dispute about who shall ride Adams's horse (which the servants have again retrieved for him and fetched with them to the inn) Fanny consents to ride pillion with Joseph and Adams accepts a ride in Pounce's coach.

During the journey, in Chapter 13 which concludes Book III, Pounce makes it clear, even to the ingenuous Adams, that he is mean, money-grubbing and actively detests any provision for the poor. When Adams underestimates Pounce's wealth at £20,000 (an enormous sum for the time, perhaps the equivalent of £500,000 today) Pounce in a paroxysm of wounded vanity and unctuous pride proclaims himself worth twice as much and then sneers at Adams's 'torn cassock'. This insult, to his calling rather than to himself, causes Adams contemptuously to leave the coach, and walk, with Fanny and Joseph, the remaining mile to Booby Hall.

Commentary
This episode, taken as a whole, involves the travellers in the most
menacing circumstances they have so far endured, taxing their
powers of physical endurance and their faith in providence to the
uttermost. This is also the juncture at which Fielding appears to sense
that the journey, which could, after all, be more or less indefinitely
prolonged, has served its purpose, in so far as the narrative is
concerned. So, from this point his grip tightens, the action speeds up,
and the novel's affinities with the more leisured progress of the
picaresque genre and with *Don Quixote* diminish.

Chapter 8, with its animated discussion of money as the root of all
evil, functions partly as a footnote to the 'roasting' scenes in Chapter
7. It is the squire's wealth, including his purchase of a seat in
Parliament and on the bench, that enables him to act, as he does,
with impunity. Fielding's introduction of a Roman Catholic priest is
interesting evidence of his fair-mindedness. Priests were generally as
much the object of hatred and suspicion in print as they were in
conversation universal scapegoats. Fielding makes his a decent, intelligent and caring person, but with his unsleeping awareness of human
fallibility he shows that neither he nor Adams is quite as capable of
rising above monetary considerations as they would like to be. The
succeeding Chapter 9, consisting as it does almost entirely of dramatic action, is couched in a rapid, running, style, less diluted with
comic extravagance than the previous bouts of fisticuffs. Although
the business of the chamber-pot (perhaps the oldest farcical prop
known to man) and the broom do verge on farce, the actual
abduction of Fanny is anything but.

Fielding is disarmingly, even, impudently, frank about Chapter 10.
It gives him a chance to offer us his view of the contemporary theatre,
which he does in appropriately dramatic form; though we must not
suppose that the views expressed on dramatists or actors are his
own.

In Chapter 11, which Fielding sardonically advises us to skip, we
have he says, a serious 'counterpart' to Chapter 10. But the title,
'calculated for the instruction and improvement of the reader' is a
giveaway; the phrase was a cliché in pious pamphlets of the day, and
plainly Fielding has his tongue firmly planted in his cheek throughout. Adams's arguments are not at all absurd, but they are as
ineffectual as they are orthodox. Real and passionate grief such as
Joseph's cannot be assuaged by dollops of philosophy or theology.

We must, of course, look ahead to Book IV, Chapter 8 for the
sequel to this passage, but we should notice how much Adams's well-
meaning but ham-fisted concern, and Joseph's futile rage and sorrow
add to their essential humanity.

The tension having been wound up by the interludes, Chapter 12
resumes the narrative. Fanny's plight and the captain's cruelty are re-
emphasised before the rescue. It is worth noticing how Fielding

declines the opportunity for a long-drawn-out, luxuriant reunion between Joseph and Fanny; the very kind of scene which Richardson would have milked to its last drop of sentiment. Instead, the glaring contrast between Adams and Pounce is instituted, initially in physical terms. Indeed, we are given so meticulously absurd a catalogue of Adams's attire, right down to the inside-out wig, that we can hardly fail to smile. So does the normally ice-cold Pounce, which brings us to the question of motive. We may laugh at what we love, Pounce laughs at what he despises as 'someone to whom he might communicate his grandeur'. We can hear echoes of Pounce's satanic rationalisations today easily enough. 'Believe me, the distresses of mankind are mostly imaginary, and it would be rather folly than goodness to relieve them.' Sentiments not really dissimilar can still be heard even at international level, and Adam's magisterial reply 'Sure, sir, hunger and thirst, cold and nakedness, and other distresses which attend the poor, can never be said to be imaginary evils', should perhaps be inscribed over the entrance to the United Nations buildings. Fielding's mordant and cutting style is at its best in Pounce's reply. 'How can any man complain of hunger in a country where such excellent salads are to be gathered in almost every field?' a sentence worthy of the master satirist Jonathan Swift. Adams's contemptuous departure fittingly concludes the Book, not at all spoiled in its effect by his forgetting his hat.

Book IV

Chapters 1–3. Summary
Lady Booby arrives by coach just as Adams, Fanny, and Joseph, warmly welcomed by the whole village, enter the parish. Her ardour for Joseph, which she is endeavouring to quench by a sojourn in the country, is instantly rekindled, and she again regrets her precipitate dismissal of him, over which, back in London, she has had another slanging match with Mrs Slipslop. She is therefore infuriated to hear Adams read, for the first time of asking, his protégé's banns in church, summons him to attend her, and attempts to browbeat him into refusing to repeat the banns (which required three readings before the wedding could be solemnised). He proves immovable, despite her threats to have 'the doctor' (i.e. the incumbent or Rector of the parish, to whom, as curate, Adams is answerable) sack him. But Adams, secure in the belief that his first duty is to God, cannot be shifted, so she sends for 'Lawyer' Scout, an unqualified but plausible 'quack' solicitor who agrees, for a fee, to contrive some means of bringing Joseph and Fanny before Justice Frolick. This venal magistrate will readily pervert justice to serve Lady Booby's ends, says Scout, including committing the lovers to Bridewell (gaol) for some triviality, where they will probably starve or die of disease.

The chapter ends with Fielding's heartfelt condemnation of such impostors as Scout.

Commentary

Note. Book IV, besides dispensing with an introductory chapter, continues and increases the rapidity and profusion of incident already apparent towards the end of Book III. As the climax of the narrative approaches, action largely takes over from discussion, nearly all of it hinging on the varied obstructions which emerge to the match between Joseph and Fanny, so that the theme of Book IV might be summed up in the well-worn quotation, 'The course of true love never did run smooth' (*A Midsummer Night's Dream*, I, i).

Chapters 1–3

These three chapters, taken together, chart the emergence of Lady Booby as the principal menace to the happiness of Joseph, Fanny and Adams; a menace in some respects worse than those they encountered on the journey, in that her enmity is calculated and unceasing, while she has wealth and influence at her command. Except that she is so impenetrably selfish, we could almost feel some sympathy with her, so totally is she at the mercy of her feelings, running the gamut of emotions; so incapable of imagining that it is mostly simple disinclination that makes Joseph reject her advances. This, when she sends for Slipslop, conduces to black comedy, for Slipslop, with the same emotions, and equally egocentric, is not, like Lady Booby, unwilling to admit the truth about herself or her mistress.

Lady Booby's second interview, with Adams, forces her to face another kind of truth, equally unwelcome, that of limitations to her power. He is never less than courteous; it is she who reveals her overweening vanity and malevolence, all of which are, to Adams, so much water off a duck's back. Though he knows she is perfectly capable of carrying out her threats (without the 'licence', which he cannot afford to purchase from the bishop, he is without security of tenure), he is far more confident in his faith than she can ever be in her position. Indeed, his dignity, like her pettiness, becomes steadily more apparent as the interview continues; his clinching retort is a noble sentence which might have come from one of the Epistles of St Paul.

Chapter 3 gives us yet another interview, again in sharp contrast with its predecessor. This begins with a dispute and ends with a thoroughly disreputable accord between a Lady Booby now openly devoid of all scruples, and a Lawyer Scout who clearly does not know what a scruple is. Just as Adams had rested his case upon divine justice, so now Scout will base his upon human 'law' at its most perverse and corrupt. His grovelling and flattery are acidly depicted, while it is interesting to see how, even in the midst of an indefensible conspiracy, Lady Booby must still try to persuade herself, and Scout,

that her motives are commendable. In her, vanity and hypocrisy have
reached a point where she can no longer distinguish between good
and evil.

Chapters 4–6. Summary
In Chapter 4 Lady Booby's wrath is fuelled again by her hearing
Adams read the banns in church a second time, but she is at first
mollified to hear from Slipslop that Joseph and Fanny have been
arrested, and are due to appear before the justice, on what charge no
one knows. Just as it is dawning on her that her scheme will dispose of
Joseph, as well as Fanny, her nephew is announced (Lady Booby's
husband was young Squire Booby's uncle) with his just-wedded wife,
Pamela (née Andrews, and Joseph's sister, of course) who is now
her niece by marriage. Squire Booby has already learnt, at his wife's
request, from the Booby Hall servants, what has happened to his
brother-in-law, and hastens to the court, where the monstrous Justice
Frolick has just sentenced Joseph and Fanny to two months in prison
on a trumped-up charge of their having stolen a twig. Luckily, the
justice knows Squire Booby and releases Joseph and Fanny into his
custody, dropping the charge against them. The squire fits Joseph out
in a suit of his own clothes, without revealing his reasons, and returns
to Fanny, whom the dreadful Frolick is now making up to with a view
to seducing her. He takes her and Joseph back to Booby Hall in his
coach, picking up Adams on the way, and explains, *en route*, the
consequences for Joseph of their new relationship. When he repeats
this to his aunt, she is secretly delighted at this apparently heaven-
sent chance to renew her assault on Joseph's virtue, happy to
welcome him, but obdurately refuses to receive Fanny as his fiancée,
or in any capacity whatever. Joseph is with difficulty prevailed upon
to remain and Fanny is glad to go to stay with the Adams family
nearby.

Joseph relates his adventures since leaving London to the Booby
family, provoking both Lady Booby's and his sister's jealousy of
Fanny's beauty, to which Squire Booby is also susceptible. The
Boobys prevail on him to stay overnight, but he is off to see his Fanny
very early next day, and arranges, with Adams, to marry her on the
next Monday. Meanwhile, overnight, Lady Booby has sung Joseph's
praises at length to her confidante Slipslop, who, well aware of her
mistress's intentions, suggests she employ Scout again, this time to
dispose of Fanny. Lady Booby affects to be offended at this slur on
her honour and rounds upon Slipslop as usual, but in the end listens
placidly to Slipslop's own eulogy of Joseph's charms.

Commentary
Apart from Fielding's delicious aside on Lady Booby as having no
'vice inconsistent with good breeding' Chapter 4 simply promotes the
action. In Chapter 5 we are treated to the last of Fielding's court

scenes. The young squire's horror at the notion of sending two people to prison for the theft – if indeed the whole incident is not fabricated – of a 'twig', and Scout's perfectly correct assertion that calling it a 'young tree' would have made the offence punishable by death both testify, like many preceding episodes, to Fielding's angry conviction that the law, as it then stood, was 'an ass'. His wish to see it reformed did not wholly arise from humanitarian motives; the existing system, apart from its barbaric punishments, was often unworkable. Capital punishment, when one could be hanged for such trivialities, was no deterrent; the proverb 'One might as well be hanged for a sheep as a lamb', was then a simple statement of fact. Juries, naturally, refused to find those accused guilty, in many cases.

Thus Justice Frolick, although a monster, illiterate, unashamedly corrupt, ready to procure Fanny as his mistress, and given to sadism in his taste for 'stripping and whipping' is not by any means an incredible caricature. He is rather an expression of Fielding's loathing for the distortion of the common law (before which every man was theoretically equal), into an instrument of tyranny and oppression. Squire Booby (and here no doubt Fielding deliberately chose to depart from Richardson's vicious Mr B, however much 'reformed' by Pamela) is an amiable and sensible young man, not very remarkable, but typical of his class.

In Chapter 6 an unholy alliance is formed between Lady Booby and Pamela who share a capacity for jealousy of Fanny's beauty, though they still manage to detest each other. But Fielding only touches in Pamela. He could obviously not have brought his bawdy strumpet Shamela into this book, yet he can equally have had no wish to present her as Richardson's paragon of all the graces. She is accordingly kept in the background. Fielding's gift for the two-edged remark is delightfully apparent when Lady Booby, singing her own praises, says of her late, lamented husband. 'All the time I ever cohabited with him, he never obtained even a kiss from me without my expressing reluctance in the granting of it'. No wonder, we feel, 'he never suspected how much [she] loved him'.

Chapter 7. Summary

Fielding begins with a sustained reflection, prompted by Lady Booby's self-deceiving antics, on the force of habit, and in particular those damaging habits instilled into girls from an early age via continual warnings of the dangers to be anticipated from men. These ultimately produce a state of mind in which women are deluded into supposing themselves to detest those very men with whom they are really in love, as witness Lady Booby with Joseph. Lady Booby persuades her nephew to attempt to dissuade Joseph from his marriage to Fanny, and this he attempts to do, on the ground that, with Joseph's elevation to a higher rank of society it would be an injudicious match, damaging to his prospects and offensive to his relations. Joseph, at first politely, dissents, and is at last provoked into reminding his brother-in-law that this is a case of the pot calling the kettle black, at which point the discussion ends amidst general annoyance.

Fanny, coming to meet Joseph, encounters first a mounted 'beau' (actually Beau Didapper who is introduced in Chapter 9), whose sexual advances she is able to repel, but whose servant, whom he has left behind to attempt further persuasion, attempts to rape her. Joseph, however, arrives at their tryst, and, after a fierce battle, knocks her assailant out, after which he escorts her back to the Adams's house where she is staying.

Commentary

This longer than average chapter divides into three sections. The first adds to our knowledge of Fielding's insight into human psychology his perception that what we would call 'acquired characteristics', including prejudices of course, are often irrevocably planted in children by unthinking adults. The second section gains in ironic force if we remember that exactly those arguments that Squire Booby deploys against Joseph's proposed marriage might, with a good deal more relevance, have been urged against his own to Pamela, who now feels herself miraculously transformed by her wedding into a superior person. The cogency and firmness of Joseph's conduct of his side of the argument are notable; neither his manners nor his speech are in the least inferior to the squire's. This is part of Fielding's plan of course; Joseph matures steadily through the book, if perhaps a trifle more rapidly than the time scale warrants.

The arrival on the scene of Beau Didapper heralds a new variation on affectation; we have not so far been privileged to meet a male specimen of the 'beau monde'. Didapper is a thinly masked portrait of John, Lord Hervey, an immensely wealthy, foppish, sycophantic hanger-on and agent of Sir Robert Walpole, the 'great man' and – for many years – Prime Minister. Fielding here breaks for once with his sound rule of avoiding personal attacks, though Hervey *was* pretty generally detested.

Chapters 8–9. Summary

Parson Adams's wife, afraid that her husband's obduracy will spoil her plans to advance her children via Lady Booby's influence, tries hard to divert him from supporting Joseph's intention to marry Fanny, but without avail. Joseph and Fanny arrive and Joseph, disturbed by the recent assault on Fanny and made uneasy by Squire Booby's efforts to discourage him from marrying her, demands a special licence (which would have allowed an immediate wedding). Adams persuades him to wait until the banns have been called. He then rehearses his wedding sermon for Joseph's benefit and ends by rebuking him for entertaining so strong a passion for Fanny that he would not willingly relinquish her, even to God, asserting that a true Christian ought to be prepared to resign anything or anyone to 'God's providence' without complaint. At this juncture he is distracted by the news that his youngest son has been drowned, and all Joseph's attempts to console him by reiterating Adam's own recent advice on Christian fortitude and resignation fall on deaf ears, until Adams is transported with delight to learn that the same poor pedlar who had earlier lent him money to extricate himself from debt (Book II, Ch. 16) has now rescued his son from the river. After dancing around the room with joy Adams immediately resumes his discourse to Joseph on the inadvisability of 'giving way' to the passions, at which even his good-natured protégé cannot refrain from reminding the parson that there is some obvious discrepancy between his professions and his practice. Adams is not disconcerted, but makes the mistake of saying that men should love their wives with 'moderation', to which his wife takes angry, and well-argued, exception.

Her harangue is interrupted by the arrival, at the start of Chapter 9, of Lady Booby, who, in furtherance of her design to promote Beau Didapper's fancy for Fanny (and thereby her own desire for Joseph) brings her visitors to call at the Adams's cottage. Though Mrs Adams is deferential, Adams disconcerts Didapper by quoting Horace at him, whose supposition that the Latin must be Welsh is the signal for Fielding to begin another ruthless dissection of his character in which his (or rather Hervey's) grovelling dependence on 'the great man' (i.e. Walpole) is again underlined. After some fatuous 'witty' exchanges between Lady Booby and the Beau, Adams is persuaded to allow his youngest son, Dick, to read aloud.

The 'improving' tale he embarks on forms Chapter 10, and in so far as it has a point at all, it concerns the difficulties experienced by an impoverished young man called Paul, who inadvisedly takes up his residence with his married friend Leonard, and gradually becomes a kind of living-in referee in the endless disputes about trivialities which occur between Leonard and his wife. The tale stops short at the outset of Chapter 11, where Didapper, who has so far confined himself to words in his unwelcome attentions to Fanny, now essays action, whereupon Joseph deals him a hefty box on the ear. Didapper draws his sword and frightens the ladies with his cursing, Adams picks up a saucepan-lid as a shield and Joseph his cudgel, at which point Fanny faints. Squire Booby now contrives to pacify the (theoretically) warlike Didapper, and then, assisted by Lady Booby, and – for her own reasons – Mrs Adams, renews the attack upon Joseph for his obdurate determination to marry Fanny, while Pamela turns on the distraught Fanny for her presumption in wishing to marry into the Booby family. At this, Joseph angrily disclaims any

wish to continue his relationship with his new-found kin, and takes
Fanny out. The Boobys and their guests depart, whereupon Mrs
Adams and her eldest daughter take Adams to task for having
defended Joseph at the risk of ruining his own family's prospects. The
jealous daughter's spiteful assertion that she would give nothing to
Fanny even if she were starving is handsomely countered by Dick's
offer of all he has – a scrap of bread and cheese. The family dispute is
interrupted by the return of Joseph, Fanny and the pedlar, who, with
all the Adams family, is invited to dinner at the 'George' inn by
Joseph.

Commentary
Chapter 8, with Adams's lengthy discourse to Joseph on the need to
'subdue the passions', needs careful consideration, as not only does it
look backward to Book III, Chapter 9, but also forward to the
revelation of Joseph's apparent relationship with Fanny in Chapter
12. It is, of course, in part comical. It inverts the situation where
Adams was ineptly trying to console Joseph for Fanny's abduction
and likely rape, albeit it only becomes comical when we learn of
Dick's rescue. But there is more to this than an amusing reversal of
roles, and it would be particularly silly to suppose that Fielding
intends us to see Adams here as being like John Bunyan's Mr Facing-
both-ways (in *The Pilgrim's Progress*). In fact, what he says to Joseph
is, from the point of view of Christian doctrine, perfectly orthodox,
while his own belief in it is unquestionable. Yet, what would we think
of him if Adams were to act in strict accordance with his reiterated
doctrines? It is precisely because his love and grief for his son, and his
uninhibited delight at his rescue, burst out in tears and laughter, that
we feel him to be a man like ourselves. If theology promotes
inhumanity, so much the worse for theology, would seem to be
Fielding's position. That 'overflowing of a full, honest open heart'
which Adams displays, is alluded to in the chapter heading where we
are told 'some few readers' will think it 'very low, absurd and
unnatural.' People like Peter Pounce have this 'control' over their
feelings. Didapper displays, as Fielding says, 'moderation' in his
passions, Lady Booby's grief for her husband's death is so well
subdued that she is playing cards and giving Joseph the come-hither
within a week of his death. These are not models we should emulate,
surely?

The point is that Fielding here acutely discriminates between the
appearance and the reality of the three great emotions; passionate
love, genuine grief and uninhibited gratitude and invites us to make
our own judgement upon them. The basis for forming those judge-
ments is, in a sense, what the whole book is about; as affectation
includes a consistent effort to appear better than one really is, so,
paradoxically, the lack of it may often make a person appear worse

than he is. It is how we act, not what we profess, that entitles us to, or denies us, acceptance as fully human beings.

It is hard to know what to say of Chapter 10. I suppose it is just possible it is a leg-pull, part of the fun-and-games aspect of Fielding's art, parodying the tedious moralising tales then thought appropriate for young readers. It is otherwise hard to account for something so flat and pointlessly repetitive.

Chapter 11 again throws into relief the warmth and depth of feeling shared by Joseph and Adams and so notably lacking in Mrs Adams's guests. Fielding skilfully conveys the confused babble and uproar, and little Dick's innocent charity towards Fanny, with his sister's reaction, neatly restates the point that envy and malice often masquerade as morality. Nevertheless Dick's precocious appreciation of Fanny's good looks, and Mrs Adams's application of 'matrimonial balsam' – a delicious phrase – keep the novel firmly rooted in reality. It is his employment of a continuous flux of such small, sharply observed, details that enables Fielding to avoid any appearance of mounting a soap-box to harangue his readers.

Chapters 12–13. Summary
In Chapter 12, as they walk to the inn, the pedlar confides that he can tell Fanny (until now thought to be a foundling) about her parentage. He says that he was told, by his gipsy-bred common-law wife (on her deathbed), that her tribe had practised child-stealing. It lies heavily on her conscience that she, though only once, herself stole a child, an exceptionally beautiful girl, who – two years after her abduction – had been sold to the late Sir Thomas Booby for three guineas. The child, now revealed as Fanny, had been taken from the home of the Andrews family, who, the pedlar's wife recalled, had another daughter, named Pamela. This apparently irrefutable evidence that Joseph must be Fanny's brother leaves everyone thunderstruck, and – but for Adam's jealous daughter – grief-stricken.

In Chapter 13 we return to Lady Booby, once more tormented by lust for Joseph, despair at his indifference and jealousy of Fanny. Slipslop adds fuel to the flame by encouraging her mistress to consider that, whatever public opinion may say, it is now feasible for her to marry Joseph, if only Fanny can be disposed of, adding that Didapper intends to abduct her that very night. She leaves Lady Booby torn between her snobbish aversion to marrying a footman, and her undiminished desire for Joseph's 'person', only to return hotfoot with the (to Lady Booby) welcome news, that Joseph is found to be Fanny's brother. Her qualms of conscience immediately dissipated, Lady Booby hastens to pass on the information to Pamela and her nephew. Pamela angrily refuses to accept it, contending that she and Joseph were her parents' only children, which naturally enrages Lady Booby. The squire patches up a truce, sends for all concerned, and hears the story again. He then asks everyone to defer any final verdict until next day, when the Andrews parents are due to arrive, he having sent a coach for them already.

Commentary
Chapter 12 can be briefly dealt with. It shows Fielding's grasp of close-packed narrative. Although he does allow himself one joke when Adams says, innocently 'Yes – there are several Boobys who are squires', he is primarily concerned to wind up the pace of the action as the novel approaches its climax. Chapter 13 is, accordingly the last of those which are even partly discursive, commencing, after a little of Slipslop's crafty advice, with one of Lady Booby's now familiar soliloquies. As this is the last of them it is a good moment to point out that they all have a triple purpose. First of all, in their impossibly artificial and operatic language – 'Ha! and do I doat thus upon a footman. I despise, I detest my passion!' – they deride the 'heroic tragedies' and popular 'romances' of Fielding's time. Neither to themselves, nor to others, do people express themselves in this way. Lady Booby here is strongly reminiscent of Glumdalca (in Fielding's splendid burlesque *The Life and Death of Tom Thumb*, 1730). Secondly, though her language is more restrained, Pamela was also addicted to such prolonged self-analyses, having no one else to confide in. Lastly, irrespective of her conscience's promptings, Lady Booby always does just what she wants, so that these internal debates are really only a kind of spiritual tranquiliser, without long-term or even short-term efficacy. It is, Fielding implies, of no significance how often we 'examine' our motives as long as we please ourselves in our actions. Goodness does not need to take thought.

Chapter 14. Summary
This self-contained episode hinges upon Beau Didapper's abortive attempt to sneak into Fanny's bed, masquerading as Joseph, in the small hours. He actually leaps naked into Slipslop's, unable (because fully curtained four-posters were pitch dark within) to see who its occupant is. His talent for mimicry has persuaded Slipslop that he is Joseph, and though both realise their error she, unlike Didapper, is perhaps ready to accept second best, but, when he tries to elude her, she is piqued and shrieks for help. Adams rushes in stark naked to the rescue and in the gloom supposes, from Didapper's effeminate physique, that he is female, and from her 'rough beard' that Slipslop is the assailant, allowing the Beau to depart. He tries to pinion Slipslop, who cuffs him and their ensuing struggles, interspersed by her cries that she is a woman, are interrupted by a candle-bearing Lady Booby, who promptly accuses the flabbergasted Adams of debauching Slipslop. Adams, modestly taking shelter in Slipslop's bed, attempts explanations, without effect until Lady Booby spots Didapper's discarded clothes on the floor and all is explained and forgiven.

Lady Booby departs and Slipslop's goodwill towards Adams is so apparent that he, in desperate haste to evade her, accidentally gets into Fanny's bed and falls asleep there, only to be discovered next morning by the thunderstruck Joseph who has come to wake her. Though this confusion too is resolved, Adams persists in suspecting that witchcraft is behind the events.

Commentary
As this is the most sustained comic passage in the novel, I have treated it in some detail, so that it will serve as a companion piece to 7 (Analysis of Book i, Ch. 12).

This chapter closely resembles stage farce, where visual, as well as verbal, humour figures largely. To make us 'see' what happens Fielding employs something like stage directions, expressed in a style of almost breathless rapidity because, if the audience had time to reflect, the essential unlikelihood of the events would become blatant. The four-poster (such beds always had heavy encompassing curtains) is an ingenious 'prop'. Without 'a glimpse of light' Didapper's error is made plausible, though, because any real apprehension that Fanny is there would spoil his effect, Fielding signals the truth to us by the 'savour' which 'invaded [Didapper's] nostrils'.

Accordingly we can relish Didapper's (obviously prepared) speech as a prelude to his discomfiture, while such phrases as 'embraced his angel' and 'great rapture' add a spice of absurdity. The anticipated 'double-take' effect, which the cinema has made familiar, follows, but not quite as usual. Didapper's 'hug' is 'returned with equal ardour', and we now realise whom Slipslop supposes she has embraced. Fielding now turns to verbal humour, deploying his gift for sarcastic epithets like 'the *watchful* Slipslop', 'that *prudent* woman', 'wonderful *presence of mind*', ironically suggesting his approval of her snap decision to 'make an immediate sacrifice to [rather than the expected *of*] her virtue'. This dextrous twist leads to yet another kind of comedy; cross-purposes give way to uproar, and as we hear Slipslop's protestations, which she hopes will restore her reputation for 'impregnable chastity', we envisage the rat-like half-naked Beau wriggling vainly in her iron clutch.

Chaos returns when the stark naked, ungainly form of Adams rushes in to make confusion worse confounded by releasing Didapper and setting about Slipslop. A sequence of pure slapstick ensues, pointed up by Fielding's vigorous language: 'cuffed and scratched', 'stroke on his chops', 'remembrance in the guts', Lady Booby's arrival with a candle metaphorically darkens things yet more. The tableau is splendidly envisaged, the dishevelled Slipslop, the – for once justifiably – enraged Lady Booby, the ungainly Adams over-come by modesty. The spectacle of his head, emerging from the bed-cloths with its 'flannel nightcap' adding a touch of wholly absurd domesticity, is especially delectable.

The scene concludes on a high note with Slipslop's (so unfortu-
nately phrased) explanation, 'Here may have been a dozen men in
the room', and her ever-hopeful attempt to woo Adams, of all
people. It was a foregone conclusion that he should go astray again,
and here Fielding slyly introduces a glimpse of Adams's domestic
situation to vary the comedy. The phrase 'deposited his carcase on
the bed post' sums up his relationship with his wife succinctly.

Lastly comes the comedy of anticipation, for the reader has been
carefully prepared for the closing absurdities of Adams's discovery by
Joseph. Confusion reaches a climax with Adams's renewed obsession
with 'witchcraft' and poor Fanny's incomprehension, while there is a
final delightful turn when, Joseph's common-sense having hit on the
true explanation, Adams, unabashed and cool as a cucumber, merely
comments 'Odso, that's true: as sure as sixpence you have hit on the
very thing'!

Fielding carries off the whole chapter with superb assurance, never
once declining into *telling* us what is funny or inviting us to laugh, but
keeping, throughout a long sequence of increasingly ludicrous hap-
penings, a perfectly straight face. After nearly 250 years the passage
is hilarious on a first reading, and still funny on a tenth.

Chapters 15–16. Summary
The Adams parents arrive, everyone meets to hear their account, and
Squire Booby puts it to old Mr Adams that Fanny must be his stolen
daughter, only for him to deny, like Pamela, that he ever had more
than two children. At this, the dismayed Lady Booby recalls the
pedlar, who sticks to his story, whereupon Mrs Andrews breaks down
and acknowledges Fanny as her long-lost elder daughter, born while
her husband, a soldier, was on foreign service, but for whom a 'sickly'
boy was substituted by the gipsies who stole Fanny. She brought up
Joseph as her son, and her husband naturally accepted him when he
returned, years later. Persuaded by his strawberry birth-mark (which
the pedlar's late wife adduced as evidence) that Joseph was the
substituted child and not his own, Mr Andrews still has to be
convinced by the pedlar that Fanny is his daughter. In his explanations the pedlar adds that Joseph was himself also stolen, by the same
gipsies, and exchanged because of his ill-health. Albeit Joseph came
from a good home, the pedlar cannot now recall the name of his
parents who, however, live not very far away. At this point however,
Mr Wilson's arrival is announced to Adams on whom he has come to
call, and when Adams tells him of the 'strawberry birth-mark' he
rushes in to claim Joseph as his son (of whose loss we learnt in Book
III, Chapters 3 and 4, with the matter of the birth-mark, which struck
a chord in Adams's memory). All the difficulties are now resolved,
and everyone except Lady Booby is more or less delighted by the
outcome. She departs in despair and fury, which prompts Squire

Booby to leave Booby Hall, and so, after introductions and congratu-lations all round, the entire party (apart from Lady Booby) set off by coach, accompanied by Adams on and sometimes off, his horse. They stay the night and are lavishly entertained, at Squire Booby's own residence, to which Mrs Wilson, Joseph's mother, is brought by the Squire's coach. On Sunday Adams, who has arranged to have the banns read in their home parish for the last time, marries Joseph and Fanny in the local church and Squire Booby lays on a splendid feast.

After Joseph and Fanny have enjoyed a brief honeymoon, Mr Wilson takes them home with him. Joseph, with a dowry Squire Booby has generously given Fanny, buys a small estate adjacent to his father's and the Squire also presents Mr Adams to a good living. The pedlar is found a post as an exciseman and Lady Booby consoles herself with a Captain of Dragoons in London, while the others dwell happily in the country with no wish to see the city again.

Commentary
The arrival of the Andrews ('*Gaffar*' and '*Gammar*' are affectionate contractions for Grandfather and Grandmother) is of course the dramatic crux of the narrative and Fielding cleverly utilises the rather rambling and diffuse narrative of old Mrs Andrews to clinch his plot. He dextrously prolongs the tension by the business of the birth-mark, Adams's half-recollection (a challenge to the reader, of course) and finally Mr Wilson's decidedly on-cue arrival. To the relatively sophisticated modern reader these successive twists may seem clichés; to Fielding's original audience they were strikingly fresh and ingenious no doubt. He declines the temptation to wallow in senti-mentality, the last chapter is full of warmth but not gush, ties up all the threads neatly and plausibly, inserts one sardonic little squib in the 'greatly beloved' status of the pedlar as 'exciseman' (the only customs officials who were liked were those who turned a blind eye to smugglers), and ends with a final encomium of the rural life which echoes Pope's often quoted lines:

> Happy the man whose wish and care
> A few paternal acres bound,
> Content to breath his native air,
> In his own ground.
> (*Ode on Solitude*, 1717)

4 THEMES

4.1 INTRODUCTION

In his *Author's Preface*, and in Book I, Chapter 1, Fielding has firmly indicated what his over-riding concern in *Joseph Andrews* is to be. His dominant theme is 'affectation'. Fielding is careful to discriminate between that variety of affectation which arises from vanity, is often quite unconscious and may be pretty harmless (like, say, Adams's persuasion that he was himself 'the greatest of all schoolmasters', Book III, Chapter 5) though it is often absurd to the onlooker, and that variety which is the outcome of hypocrisy. This kind is calculated in that it deliberately sets out to falsify and deceive, and is therefore always reprehensible and often wicked.

Fielding, of course, offers us numerous and variegated instances of affectation in all its forms. The critical commentary identifies many as they occur in the narrative. They range from the trivial – like the squabble between Adams and the inn-keeper who was once at sea, the one proud of his reading, the other of his travel – to the monstrous; Justice Frolick's 'affectation' of kindly concern for Fanny is an instance.

But it may be helpful to consider how far Fielding is following a highly traditional moral order. It is true that the concept of the Seven Deadly Sins is medieval rather than scriptural, but it formed a prominent part of the preacher's stock-in-trade until some way into the nineteenth century. The traditional list was as follows: Pride/Wrath or Hate/Lechery or Lust/Envy/Sloth/Avarice or Covetousness/Gluttony. Pride always came first and Pride is, of course, the root of both affectation and hypocrisy. In their various ways all the more unpleasant characters exhibit pride, Lady Booby, Slipslop, Pounce, Pamela, and 'high people' generally. Indeed, everyone has it in some degree, Adams is proud of his skills as preacher and teacher, Joseph of his talent for riding. But each of the other categories is clearly represented. Mrs Tow-wouse is Wrath personified, Hatred is displayed in the maligant squire who first baits Adams and then tries to abduct Fanny. Lady Booby and Didapper represent Lechery, Mrs Slipslop and Adams's jealous daughter, Envy. Parson Barnabas (who has no sermon ready just before the funeral) and the inn-keeper (who has never concerned himself about death and judgement) are instances of Sloth. Pounce, of course, and Leonora's father (in Book II, Ch. 6) are archetypes of Avarice, as is Trulliber of Gluttony. I do not infer that Fielding deliberately set out to follow such a scheme. It is, however, obvious that Joseph, Adams and Fanny embody the seven opposed or 'corrective' virtues. But, though they do display Humility, Patience, Chastity, Charity, Industry, Generosity and Abstinence most of the time, none of them manages a uniform adherence to these principles. Fielding, I suggest, thought that would be too much to hope for, that it would be incredible (just as Pamela's invincible rectitude was incredible to him) except in a saint.

4.2 THE 'CHRISTIAN HERO'

The mention of saints, however, leads naturally to a matter which critics have frequently disputed. The essayist, Sir Richard Steele (1672–1724) had written, in 1701, a highly influential pamphlet entitled *The Christian Hero*. In it he declared that '. . . no principles but those of religion are sufficient to make a great man'. This sparked off a good deal of discussion. Attempts were made both in fiction and drama to create Christian heroes and heroines and the *Gentleman's Magazine* (1731–1914) actually ran a competition to define such a hero. Now the idea that 'It is hard to be good' is as old as written literature; the corollary that it is exceedingly difficult to portray goodness plausibly is of more recent growth. Literature is full of abortive attempts. Richardson's interminable and unreadable *Sir Charles Grandison* (1754) is one, Steele's own play *The Conscious Lovers* is another. Of it, Adams says (Book III, Chapter 11) '. . . there are some things [in it] almost solemn enough for a sermon'. There Fielding mockingly reveals his awareness of the problems inherent in turning novel or stage into a pulpit. There are two capital difficulties, in fact. The first arises from the all-too-evident gulf between precept and practice which those who are professionally 'required' to be good too frequently display. Fielding was no complaisant admirer of the clergy. Aside from Adams all those who are on show in *Joseph Andrews* are, to say the least, poor models for their parishioners to emulate. They constitute a counterpoise to the rectitude which Adams displays, and thereby prevent the book from turning into a 'commercial' for the Established Church.

The other difficulty lies in the nature of Christian behaviour; in the manifestation of the cardinal virtues listed above. It is hard to convey them in literary terms without their seeming negative. A series of temptations declined, of challenges rejected, does not make for much excitement or – after a chapter or two – much narrative tension either.

It is to guard against this risk that Fielding offers us a Christian Hero with a difference, in Adams supplemented by the more muted picture of Joseph. For, whatever emollient qualities Adams may lack – and how many congregations today would be entirely at ease with him as their minister? – he is anything but passive or negative in action or when some tough moral issue has to be decided, although, and this is a subtle touch, he can be prosaically pious on occasion. He is the active principle of virtue in the book and if not precisely a model for us to emulate – that would be more true of Joseph, perhaps – he is a standing reproach to formal and conventional religious observance, heartless piety and humbug generally. The answer to the question then, 'Did Fielding attempt to depict a Christian Hero?' is 'Yes!', but with the qualification that few readers of his own day would have recognised or accepted him as such. Judging, as they mostly would have done, by externals, they would have perceived him as no credit to the church at all.

4.3 'ILLUSION AND REALITY'

One of the things which makes Adams so vivacious and engaging is certainly something of a disqualification for his function as Joseph's mentor in the business of everyday life. As Fielding makes plain from the start, he invariably believes what he is told, frequently rejecting the evidence of his senses and even of his common-sense – with which he is not superabundantly endowed anyway – in favour of whatever seems the more agreeable interpretation of the facts. Adams is not, of course, alone in his preference for the ideal to the real but this is where Joseph, whose common-sense is very strongly marked, and increases as he learns from experience, comes into his own. Alone among the major characters of the book, he does not prefer his own version of life as it might be to life as it is. It bears upon Fielding's concern with affectation, in that those who display vanity and even hypocrisy are indicating their preference for an ideal version of themselves. One of Fielding's contemporaries, Bishop Joseph Butler (1692 – 1752) wrote, grimly: 'Things and actions are what they are, and the consequences of them will be what they will be: why then should we desire to be deceived?' But, as Fielding well knew, we all do, and a sharp awareness of this paradox underlines his portrayal of men and women in *Joseph Andrews*.

4.4 MINOR THEMES

In addition to those major concerns I have outlined above, there are other recurring interests in *Joseph Andrews*. Fielding, who had had to display almost superhuman powers of concentration and determination himself to qualify as a barrister, was, naturally, both sensitive and well-informed on the whole subject of the law and lawyers. The English common law he perceived as an often imperfect, sometimes corrupt, occasionally absurd instrument of justice. But, with all its weaknesses, it was the *only* instrument then available to protect men from the ravages of other men. (There was no police force, only village constables and the Watch in London, both 'amateur' and usually ineffectual.) Accordingly, Fielding devotes a fair amount of space to the castigation of lawyers, from the self-seeking professionalism of the one in the coach (Book I, Ch. 12), the asinine antics of the 'amateurs' Barnabas and the surgeon (Book I, Ch. 15) through the prejudiced and blinkered conduct of the two in Book II, Chapter 3, the unprincipled soliciting of the 'gentleman' in Book II, Chapter 5, and all the way down hill to the wretched and iniquitous quackeries of Scout in Book IV, Chapter 3. The local Justices of the Peace come off no better. On the one hand we have the fuddled blend of ignorance and prejudice of the Justice in Book II, Chapter 11 and on the other that kedgeree of all the vices which Fielding savagely entitled Justice Frolick in Book IV, Chapter 8. All in all, it is a pretty depressing picture, but one not likely to have been inaccurate in its details. Of course, Fielding is not concerned to present a balanced view. His intention is corrective.

We need to be careful when we look at what Fielding made of the clergy in Joseph Andrews. Such men as Trulliber, the time-serving Barnabas and the sycophantic parson in Book II, Chapter 11, who is unwilling to admit his ignorance of Greek, are not meant to be representative any more than Adams himself. Nevertheless, they do constitute an indirect indictment of the church as well as a sharply critical glance at some churchmen. With exceptions, the clergy were often pitifully poor. There were many good men who were driven to choose between exercising their proper pastoral function and living at subsistence level. Then, the more or less arbitrary powers of the bishops to ordain whomsoever they pleased, and the equally unchecked power of many landowners to 'present' their own nominees to vacant livings, together with the practice of 'pluralism' (one 'rector' drawing the income from several livings and paying 'curates', like Adams, a pittance to discharge his duties in most, or even all of them) combined to make life very hard for the clergyman who had no friends in high places. Fielding was a convinced, if not conventionally devout, Anglican. Therefore, his strictures are not directed against religion, but against religiosity, the 'affectation of belief'. He concluded his essay of 1740 *An Apology for the Clergy* with an observation which summarises his position in *Joseph Andrews* too. A 'bad clergyman is the worst of men' he says, because 'if not an idiot, he *must* be an unbeliever, and a hypocrite'.

Finally, he employs *Joseph Andrews* at times as platform for his critical opinions on the novel, of course. Where he does this overtly, as in the Preface, and in the opening chapters of Books I–III, no remark is needed beyond what may be found in the Commentary. But it is worth just pointing out that the recurrent sly prods at Richardson, which are also noted as they occur in the Commentary, are likewise an indirect way of advancing Fielding's conception of what a novel *should* be.

We shall not get very far if we attempt to discover hidden meanings in *Joseph Andrews*. Fielding knew very well what he was about and said so at the outset. What he delivers is very much what he promises, a many-faceted survey of the ridiculous, of man with his motives improperly exposed, offset by one 'character of perfect simplicity' in Adams, and another of sterling good sense and unexceptional decency in Joseph.

To conclude, the passage of two and a half centuries has also turned *Joseph Andrews* into a wonderfully vivid and authoritative panorama of life along the highways in the mid-eighteenth century but that accidental addition to its value should not distract us from the continuing relevance of Fielding's remark upon his 'lawyer' (by whom he plainly meant a composite of the various individual portraits). He asserts that

The lawyer is not only alive, but hath been so these four thousand years . . . when the first mean selfish creature appeared upon the human stage, who made self the centre of the whole creation, would give himself no pain, incur no danger, advance no money, to assist or preserve his fellow-creatures; then was our lawyer born; and, whilst such a person as I have described exists on earth, so long shall he remain upon it.

Unless we choose to live in cloud cuckoo land we must concede the truth of that minatory statement. That, in a nutshell, is what Joseph Andrews is *about*. As Shakespeare put it in *Measure for Measure*

> Man, proud man
> Dressed in a little brief authority
> Most ignorant of what he's most assured,
> His glassy essence, like an angry ape
> Plays such fantastic tricks before high heaven,
> As make the angels weep.
>
> Act II, Scene ii

5 CHARACTERISATION

What has just been said about Fielding's lawyers will help the reader to understand why I have juxtaposed this section and the preceding one. Fielding states, quite unequivocally, in Book III, Chapter 1: 'I declare here, once for all, I describe not men, but manners, not an individual but a species.' If what we mean by character then, is the depiction of an individual with 'all its minute sinuousities, its depths and its shallows' – which was Sir Walter Scott's description of Richardson's treatment of characterisation – we shall not find much of it in *Joseph Andrews*. And Richardson himself, writing to Fielding's sister (after Fielding's death) to compare her novel with her brother's work, said, 'His [Fielding's] was but as the knowledge of the outside of a clockwork machine, while yours was that of all the finer springs and movements inside.' Aside from what it reveals of Richardson's unsleeping malice – he hated Fielding in spite of the admiration his rival had publicly expressed for *Clarissa* – the seeds are sown here of a long running critical debate about the nature of the novel generally, about whether the novelist should concern himself primarily with the 'journey within' like, say, Jane Austen, George Eliot and Henry James or with the 'journey without' like Smollett, Dickens and Thackeray.

Accordingly I shall take as a starting point E. M. Forster's now classic distinction between two kinds of 'people' in his *Aspects of the Novel*, 1927. He does not allow himself to make a value judgement on the two modes of approach, contenting himself with observing that '. . . people in a novel *can* be understood completely by the reader, *if the novelist wishes*; their inner as well as their outer life can be exposed' (my italics). Fielding does not so wish; the only person into whose mind we are allowed to penetrate is Lady Booby and that is neither a revelatory nor an uplifting experience.

We must accept that, by intent, nearly all Fielding's characters fit neatly into the category Forster defines as 'flat', that they are 'in their perfect form constructed around a single idea or quality'. Trulliber springs to mind with his 'I caaled vurst', Mrs Tow-Wouse with her 'Common charity a fart'. It was also, and designedly, a consequence of Fielding's intention to treat the theme of affectation in the 'manner of Cervantes' that he should depict a vast gallery of people, from sharply differing backgrounds, in a series of necessarily brief encounters along the road. Only in the confined location of a Richardsonian novel would it have been possible to 'dive into the recesses of the human heart' as Dr Johnson put it when comparing the two authors. The constraints of the form imposed by Fielding's 'model', his declared purpose to play a series of variations on the theme of affectation, his experience in the theatre, and, perhaps most importantly, his natural bent for the broad canvas rather than the miniature, all contribute to making a rapid succession of 'flat' characters inevitable.

But it is of the greatest importance to remind ourselves that Forster, by 'flat' did not mean to signify 'thin' or 'dull'. On the contrary he contends that such characters are a great 'convenience for the author, when he can strike with his full force at once', that they are 'easily remembered by the reader' and moreover 'provide their own atmosphere'. All these advantages certainly accrue to Fielding; the excoriating impact of the 'postilion . . . since transported for robbing a hen-roost', the surely unforgettable Mrs Tow-wouse with her proud self-analysis, 'If the devil was to contradict me, I would make the house too hot to hold him!', the air of sleazy, sly complicity that Slipslop gives off when with Lady Booby – each typifies to perfection the particular point Forster is making. Moreover, if we apply Forster's remarks to some of the characters who are rather more extensively presented, we shall see that Fielding was himself well aware of the gains he could expect from such intense compression and concentration. It is a critical commonplace that satire should aim to blow as large a hole as possible plumb in the centre of the target, and although *Joseph Andrews* is not, as *Shamela* was, primarily a satire, yet Fielding's aims and methods in some of his most pungently telling vignettes are satirical.

By presenting us with a portrait, merciless in its intensity, of **Justice Frolick** (his very name an upside-down indicator of his nature) Fielding simultaneously depicts injustice rampant and unashamed. We meet him first at second-hand; Lawyer Scout's testimonial is itself a guarantee of his venality and corruption: 'To say truth it is a great blessing to the country that he is in the commission [i.e. on the bench] . . . the law is a little deficient in giving us any . . . power of prevention; however, the justice will stretch it as far as he is able, to oblige your ladyship.' This is all perfectly straight-faced, uttered with the genuine warmth of admiration. The first words we hear Frolick deliver, 'No great crime . . . I have only ordered them to Bridewell for a month' are superficially quite amicable, indeed he never evinces any anger. Scout has to prompt him when the squire asks just what crime he is judging, but he is unperturbed. 'Aye', he burbles blandly, 'a kind of felonious larcenous thing. I believe I must order them a . . . little stripping and whipping'. It is as if he were reminding himself to feed the cat, and his urbane benevolence of tone accentuates the satanic malevolence of his actions throughout. His illiteracy is manifested in the 'depusition', his grovelling corruption openly avouched in the throwaway 'Lady Booby desires to get them out . . .' Finally he genially offers Fanny his 'protection'. He is as memorable as a picture by William Hogarth the artist, whose courtrooms are frequently presided over by just such depraved and grotesque monsters, and whose work Fielding much admired. The atmosphere he engenders is only fleetingly humorous (indeed Fielding, for once, directly compares Frolick with 'the devil himself'); it soon becomes repellent and disgusting.

Frolick is then perfectly flat, his responses are uniformly predictable, and in all but his role as a magistrate gone rotten, he is accordingly quite opaque to the reader. If Fielding had told us *why* he would 'willingly have sent his own wife to Bridewell', we might, just possibly, have begun to feel some understanding for him. But what was gained in insight would be lost in impact.

It is much the same case with **Peter Pounce**, though we do see more of him. We can deduce that he has fought his way up from nothing, using his native wit. His determination to succeed then, might, in itself, have been made to seem admirable, his ruthlessness as unavoidable, given his aims. But Fielding's objective is to present us with a singularly pure form of greed, only modified by an overwhelming vanity which demands flattery. This is why he tries to mask his rapacity with a thin coat of benevolence. There is no room here for sympathy, though there is room for comedy. The dialogue in Book III, Chapter 13 between him and Adams is beautifully dry. It takes Adams's ingenuousness to penetrate Pounce's assurance. There are few more telling exchanges in the book than Adams's definition of charity as ' . . . a generous disposition to relieve the distressed' and Pounce's reply 'There is something in that definition which I like well enough; it is, as you say a disposition – and does not so much consist in the act as in the disposition to do it . . .' Our acquaintance with Pounce ends with this scene, there is nothing more to be done with him, he has served Fielding's limited purposes for him and made a mark upon our minds not easily erased.

The great preponderance of Fielding's creations are, then, 'flat'. But Fielding himself excepted **Adams** from his range of 'types' as the most 'glaring', and he certainly exemplifies Forster's second category of 'rounded people'. 'The test of a rounded character', says Forster, 'is whether it is capable of surprising us in a convincing way . . . It has the incalculability of life about it . . .' Those words are more closely applicable to Adams than to anyone else, no doubt, but there are some others who cannot accurately be dismissed as altogether 'flat'. **Adams** may be left to the end, and anyone else who is not treated in this section should be looked up in the appropriate part of the Commentary.

Forster himself thought **Mrs Slipslop** was 'rounded'; I would myself add **Joseph**, while **Lady Booby**, with **Fanny**, must be included, as these five make up the quintet around whom the novel revolves in terms of its story and its plot. Except for the actual dénouement, no one else is functionally indispensable.

Superficially, the 'accomplished' Slipslop seems a grotesque of the Hogarthian variety. Harridans like her appear in *Gin Lane*, one of Hogarth's most famous pictures of drunken debauchery. Yet Fielding's gross physical portrait of her (Book 1, Ch. 6) is not the whole story. She is a curate's daughter, she has some glimmerings of an education, a fairly responsible post in the Booby household and, as we soon learn, is both observant of her mistress's real nature and crafty enough to make herself indispensable to her. Her desire for Joseph is comic, but it is also pathetic. There is never any real threat to him from her, and Fielding displays a wry, sad insight into human nature when he writes, of the thirty years she had 'continued a good maid' (i.e. a virgin), 'She imagined that by so long a self-denial . . . she had laid up a quantity of merit to excuse any future failings'. One of her rôles is to provide the reader with an image of Lady Booby with the gloves off, so to speak, and her unscrupulousness mirrors that of her mistress, as does her dexterity in rationalising her vices into virtues. But there is a touch of Chaucer's Wife of Bath in her too, and when she is cut to the quick by Lady Booby's abuse of her, 'Thou art a low creature . . . a reptile of a lower order, a weed that grows in the common garden of creation', she forgets, in her rage, to grovel and utters a number of ringing truths. 'Servants have flesh and blood as well as quality . . . I never heard Joseph say an ill word of anybody in his life . . . he is the best natured man in the world.' Aside from the comedy of her pretensions to gentility and the way in which her position as confidant points up Lady Booby's emptiness, she is also Fielding's representative of the earthy vigour of life below stairs. The speech in defence of servants just quoted, is made all the more telling by the fact that the last thing she would admit to being is a servant, and there is a splendidly rumbustious quality about some of her remarks in her last dialogue with Lady Booby (Book IV, Ch. 13). 'A fig for custom and nonsense. Shall I be afraid of eating sweetmeats because people may say I have a sweet truth? If I had a mind to marry a man, all the world should not hinder me.' Her last, undaunted attempt upon Adams's virtue 'Mrs Slipslop, with a most Christian virtue, not only forgave, but began to move with much courtesy towards him', (Book IV, Ch. 14) is entirely and delightfully typical.

Most commentators have appreciated Mrs Slipslop; **Joseph Andrews**, however, has come in for a good deal of critical stick. Phrases like 'rather pale', 'merely a pawn in the game', 'perfect and therefore not very real' are typical. The difficulty with Joseph is that first impressions are hard to erase, and our first impression of him is undeniably that of a very green young man indeed who responds first with such blank incomprehension and subsequently with such unbending rectitude to Lady Booby's ever more overt propositioning that it is difficult, subsequently, to take him seriously. We are undoubtedly meant to laugh at the rich absurdities of Book I, Chapters 5 and 8, but Fielding is not inviting us to laugh at innocence or chastity in themselves. It is probably true that Fielding did not think it very sinful to accept the advances of a beautiful woman, provided the amour did no harm to anyone else. But that is not the case here. Joseph is already, in effect, engaged to Fanny, and Lady Booby is his mistress. Apart from any natural repugnance he might feel at jumping into his late master's bed so soon after his death, he would, were he to accept her offer, become in effect a paid gigolo. For Joseph to act upon her invitation would change the whole tenor of the scene, not only demolishing the satirical pattern of references to *Pamela*, but also irremediably damaging the novel's moral structure. Fielding, in these early episodes does suffer, I think from divided aims. Thus, when Joseph robustly answers Lady Booby's attempt to put him in the wrong by urging that she is 'honouring' him 'with the highest favour in her power' he speaks with simple, colloquial force: 'I can't see why your having no virtue should be a reason against my having any . . .' If he always spoke like that, we should have no grounds for calling him 'too good to be true.' But when, with a risibly high-falutin change of diction he asserts: 'Madam . . . that boy is the brother of Pamela, and would be ashamed that the chastity of his family, which is preserved in her, should be stained in him' we see Fielding in the act of shifting his ground, and making Joseph into a lay figure for the purpose.

In fact, though only in a subdued way, Joseph does mature and develop. Once he meets his Fanny a change takes place, he begins to initiate action, he no longer simply accedes to everything Adams says, while in the analysis of Joseph's feelings in Book III, Chapter 11, when Fanny has been abducted and he is left, helpless, to suffer not only her loss but Adams's ham-fisted attempts to 'console' him, he comes fully to life. In his exchanges with Mr Booby and Pamela over his projected marriage to Fanny (Book IV, Ch. 7) he behaves with dignity and restraint, only once succumbing to the temptation to remind his brother in law of Pamela's origins. Eventually, goaded by Adams's obdurate refusal to accept his own inconsistency (Book IV, Ch. 8) he even rounds upon his mentor telling him 'It was easier to give advice than to take it', and insisting that he, even if it is 'sinful' will '. . . love without any moderation at all'. He is, of course, no namby-pamby, but quite apart from his physical strength and skill, his masculinity is also evident. There is nothing 'platonic' in his desire for Fanny. To sum up, he perhaps remains throughout rather too much of a paragon, but by Book IV he has entirely ceased to be a puppet. He can and does, stand upon his own feet.

Of **Fanny**, very little can usefully be said. She is beautiful but inarticulate, not a fragile shepherdess but a robust country girl whose physical charms indeed attract nearly everyone who sees her, but who scarcely says a word from start to finish. What we know of her is what we are told; her solitary spontaneous act is her flight to find Joseph. She is, no doubt, intended to form a total contrast with Pamela; illiterate and without formal 'accomplishments' as she is, we all know who is the more likeable. But if Fielding had, just once or twice more, allowed her some measure of self-assertion, given her an opinion or two of her own, she would have been far more animated and memorable.

Lady Booby is certainly both animated and memorable; next to Adams indeed she is the most extensively treated character in the book, albeit she only figures in Books I and IV. But if we apply Forster's test we find that she never really surprises us, once we have seen what motivates her. Fielding illustrates in her an example of what was then known as the 'ruling passion', or what we should now term 'obsessive' behaviour. In order to possess herself of Joseph, she exerts all her not inconsiderable powers of cunning and influence. But she is (in this one respect oddly akin to Adams) wholly incapable of entering imaginatively into another person's mind, and so she simply cannot conceive why Joseph should resist her blandishments. Chained to the treadmill of her own desires, her reactions are always entirely predictable. It would not have been hard for Fielding, had he wished, to have made her more sympathetic. Had she shown some real remorse for her action in dismissing Joseph, had her desire for him appeared as motivated by something more than sexuality, she might have acquired a touch of pathos. But what Fielding is really indicting, in her, is not so much wrong feeling, as total lack of feeling. Amid all her vociferous protestations: 'Ha! and do I doat thus on a footman! I despise, I detest my passion! Yet why? Is he not generous, gentle, kind? Kind to whom? . . .' she remains essentially cold, a creature of a kind Fielding particularly detested, someone masquerading as a human, without an atom of humanity, for whom repeated 'young captains of dragoons, together with endless parties at cards' constitute an empty future.

'The inimitable **Parson Adams**', says Sir Walter Scott (in his *Lives of the Novelists*, 1821) in whom 'learning, simplicity, evangelical purity of heart, and benevolence of disposition, are so admirably mingled with pedantry, absence of mind and the habit of athletic exercise' is 'one of the richest productions of the Muse of Fiction'.

Few have disagreed, whatever their views on *Joseph Andrews* as a whole, with Scott's assertion that Adams is central to the novel. Indeed, Fielding, in his use of the phrase 'glaring' (= *dazzling, prominent, dominant,* but not, as in current usage, in a derogatory sense) of Adams's character, acknowledges as much himself. He is certainly 'on stage' far longer than anyone else in the novel and there is much more to be learned of him than we might imagine from Fielding's disarmingly direct portrait in Book I, Chapter 3. Nevertheless, this succinct analysis remains valid, in essentials, throughout the book. There is a risk though, that the reader may take one sentence 'simplicity was his characteristic' in the wrong sense. Simplicity is an ambiguous term. Adams is no simpleton, but a highly intelligent and accomplished man (*good parts* = talented, accomplished). What Fielding meant by simplicity was the opposite of affectation, something Adams entirely lacks. It is not just that he is straightforward – as much can be said of Joseph – but that he is without guile. 'As he had no intention to deceive, so he never suspected such a design in others'. He thus becomes a kind of ethical litmus paper; measured against his innocent goodwill every species of affectation and hypocrisy is instantly apparent to the reader.

But, if this were his only function, he would hardly hold our interest as he does. We know he will respond with benevolence (often misplaced) and courage (sometimes misdirected)to everyone whom he encounters, yet in other respects he is perpetually and often delightfully unpredictable. Thus, in an age which set great store by the dignity of the church he appears like a 'thimble-rigger' rather than a clergyman, in a 'short white coat with black buttons, a short wig, and a hat which . . . had nothing black about it'. (He ought to have been all in black with a full wig to have qualified as 'canonically' dressed.) This happy indifference to externals extends to his behaviour too. There is nothing puritanical about his appetite for beer and good food, while he also manifests an infectious capacity for spontaneous delight, whether it be 'dancing about the room in a rapture' at Fanny and Joseph's reunion or racing a stage coach. His grief at the loss, as he supposes, of his son, is equally uncontrolled. When 'well filled with ale and pudding' at the wedding, he can even be 'facetious'.

Then there are his opinions. These are a splendid hodge-podge, ranging from the soberly orthodox '. . . no accident happens to us without the Divine permission . . . it is the duty of a man, much more of a Christian to submit' to views exuberantly, perhaps even heretically, individual. Such outbursts as his riposte to Barnabas's strictures on Whitefield light up the pages on which they appear.

'Sir,' answered Adams, 'if Mr. Whitefield had carried his doctrine no farther than you mention, I should have remained, as I once was, his well-wisher. I am, myself, as great an enemy to the luxury and splendour of the clergy as he can be. . . Surely those things, which savour so strongly of this world, become not the servants of one who professed his kingdom was not of it: but when he began to call nonsense and enthusiasm to his aid, and set up the detestable doctrine of faith against good works, I was his friend no longer; for surely, that doctrine was coined in hell, and one would think none but the devil himself could have the confidence to preach it.

The vigour, the intensity and the sheer force of his phrasing must, one feels, have made Adams's congregations less attentive to the pulpit hour-glass than most, if he spoke like this. Yet we know that he 'asserted that Mr. Adams at church with his surplice on, and Mr. Adams without that ornament in any other place, were two very different persons', so perhaps, in this as in other ways, he is inconsistent.

These contradictions extend to much of his behaviour. Though his physical courage is admirable, there is surely some relish for the battle too, as when he says to the would-be rapist, as he sits upon him and clenches his fist, 'It is my turn now!' In his own home, evidently, he rarely if ever gets the last word, but when dealing with his nominal superiors 'though he paid them all submission and deference . . . in other matters, where the least spice of religion intervened, he immediately lost all respect of persons.' It was his maxim, that he was a servant of the Highest, and could not, without departing from his duty, give up the least article of his honour, or of his cause [i.e. God's] to the greatest earthly potentate.' This is borne out by his firm, patient remonstrations with Lady Booby in Book IV, Chapter 2. It is only after enduring a long tirade of arrogance and nonsense that he concludes, with impressive, quiet dignity:

Madam . . . I know not what your Ladyship means by the terms 'master' and 'service'. I am in the service of a master who will never discard me for doing my duty, and if the doctor . . . thinks proper to turn me out from my cure, God will provide me, I hope, with another. At least, my family, as well as myself, have hands; and He will prosper, I doubt not, our endeavours to get our bread honestly with them. While my conscience is pure, I shall never fear what man can do unto me.

There is nothing remotely comic about those phrases, they have the simple force of the New Testament behind them. Yet there have been critics to label him 'a bundle of contradictions armed with a crabstick', to suggest that he is a 'caricature', a 'grotesque' of that very kind Fielding decried in his *Preface* as tending to produce 'monsters not men', 'distortions and exaggerations'.

It seems to me that Fielding saw rather more deeply into the nature of a man like Adams than the critics. To put it in a nutshell there is plenty of the old Adam in Adams, his warm, passionate nature is at odds with the cool rationality of his calling; his heart is with those men, like the Methodist Whitefield, whom his head condemns. He *thinks* that 'subordination' is proper to society, but his emotions are all on the side of the 'poor' who, he says, 'have little enough share of this world already [so that] it would be barbarous to deny [them] their common pleasures and innocent enjoyments'. He knows he ought to be pacific, but he often prefers to clinch (and sometimes to commence) his arguments with his fist. He is a powder-keg of contrary impulses, but that makes him like us, of course. As R. W. Emerson once said, 'Consistency is the hob-goblin of little minds'.

It will be helpful to conclude by referring to an essay Fielding wrote in 1740, not long before he began work on *Shamela*. In it, and after some gently ironic preliminaries, he extends the famous passage from St Paul's Epistle to the Corinthians (i, xiii) into what amounts to a code of conduct for Christians generally, and the clergy in particular. Thus he expands St Paul's 'believing all things, hoping all things' into 'weighing all mankind in the scales of friendship, and seeing them with the eyes of love'. It is the distinctive mark of Adams that he, not without incidental absurdities and disillusionments, simply does what, according to the Apostle and Fielding, we should all try to do, and in so doing becomes not only a great comic creation but a manifestation of what, at its best, human loving-kindness can attain to.

6 TECHNICAL FEATURES

6.1 HOW TO READ *JOSEPH ANDREWS*

We may as well face up directly to the fact that reading Fielding (or any of his contemporaries for that matter) is not the same sort of experience as reading a modern or even a Victorian novelist. The lapse of some 250 years, however, has had less effect than one would expect; most of the apparent difficulties arise from lack of familiarity with certain conventions. It is really no more difficult to accustom oneself to moving easily through eighteenth-century prose than it is to adjust to driving on the right in Europe. At first everything seems complicated and confusing; within an hour or so the driver will have grown used to the new rules and – although he will need to be rather more than ordinarily alert for a while – is unlikely to be baffled again. Much the same applies to reading this novel.

Nevertheless it may help the beginner to set out some of the more commonly encountered stumbling blocks quite straightforwardly. They can conveniently be divided into three categories, in ascending order of importance.

(a) Unfamiliar vocabulary.
(b) Unfamiliar syntax and conventions in orthograpy.
(c) Unfamiliar style.

Vocabulary

Only a tiny proportion of the words Fielding uses are actually obsolete. A few are rarely employed, but a good large dictionary will clear up any which the notes in your edition do not gloss. Examples from early in the book are *ratafia, green-sickness, a modus, to play booty, to asperse*. Very occasionally he will employ a word we use in a sense differing from ours; *mere*, for example in the *mere* English reader' (*The Author's Preface*) does not belittle his readers, it means they can only read English. All in all I doubt whether this kind of thing amounts to 0.01 per cent of the text.

Syntax and conventions

At a superficial glance there are a number of ways in which Fielding's handling of the language, his grammatical usage, does differ markedly from ours. He was rather an old-fashioned writer, as it happens, and so we find him employing the old forms of *hath* (for our *has*) *doth* (=does), *writ* (=written), *frighted* (=frightened), *durst not* (dare not), *whipt*(=whipped), *canst not*(=cannot), *thou art* (you are), *if you was* (=if you were) and similar archaisms. Aside from their unfamiliarity, however, these are far from obscure. Fielding also uses capital letters and commas rather more freely than we do, but in the area of punctuation there is one oddity which continually recurs. It is caused by the fact that, when Fielding wrote, the method for distinguishing direct and indirect speech was at a transitional stage. So, in the Trulliber episode (Book I, Ch. 9) we have our own mode of showing direct speech;. . . he cried out. 'Do but handle them! step in, friend!'; our own method for indirect; Her husband bid her be quiet like the fool as she was; and an in-between form where inverted commas are used where we should not employ them: Trulliber answered 'He was sorry for the mistake but that he must blame his wife . . .'. We should insert *that* before the word *He*, and omit the capital and the inverted commas. Once we recognise the convention, which continually recurs, it is obvious enough.

Style

I do not intend to deal here with the particular excellence of Fielding's prose but only with those aspects of it which it has in common with most of the work of his contemporaries; and in which it differs from today's prose.

Most obvious is the generally far greater length of Fielding's sentences, by comparison with those we are used to reading. Here is a fairly typical example – by no means the longest he employs – from *The Author's Preface*

And here I solemnly protest, I have no intention to vilify or asperse anyone; [for though] everything is copied from the book of nature [and] scarce a character or action produced which I have not taken from my own observations and experience; [yet] I have used the utmost care to obscure the persons by such different circumstances, degrees, and colours, that it will be impossible to guess at them with any degree of certainty; [and] if it ever happens otherwise, it is only where the failure characterized is so minute, that it is a foible only, which the party himself may laugh at as well as any other.

If the words in brackets are deleted, and full stops placed before, with capital letters after them, the results will show how a modern writer would, almost certainly, break this up into shorter units. Yet our being accustomed to the terser sentence is not really an argument for its superiority. It is different, that is all, and we have to learn to take a longer breath, as it were, to follow the argument.

Fielding shared to the full his age's taste for the 'balanced' sentence exhibiting a series of logical steps (signalled in the example given by phrases like *for though, and scarce, yet I have, that it will be, and if, it is only, that it is*). This manner of linking an 'argument' by conjunctions is widespread in his work. It is uncommon nowadays except in legal contexts.

Fielding also enjoyed using a device which is quite common in the Authorised Version of the Bible. It is called 'parallelism' and can be seen in action in the following sentence (where I have italicised the 'paired' or 'parallel' words and phrases)

It is a *trite* but *true* observation, that *examples* work more forcibly on the mind than *precepts*: and *if this be just* on what is *odious and blameable it is more strongly so* in what is *amiable and praiseworthy*. (Book 1, Ch. 1).

All this may seem rather stiff and formal to us but Fielding only employs this mode of writing in those contexts where he is commenting, as author, on what is taking place. Where he is concerned with either straight narrative or with dialogue, he is as brisk and lively as anyone could wish. He does, of course, treat his privilege of authorial interjection more freely than all but a few modern writers, inserting reflections or digressions whenever he feels like it, offering 'asides' to his 'readers' and using his chapter headings for the verbal equivalent of nudges and winks. But this brings us to a consideration of the particular and individual qualities that mark Fielding's work as his own, and to the end of this section.

6.2 STORY, PLOT AND STRUCTURE

Some definitions

It may be as well to distinguish, at the outset, between three terms which I employ in what follows. The *story* of Joseph Andrews, reduced to its essentials relates the progress from rags to relative riches, from adversity to happiness, of Joseph, of Fanny whom he loves, and of their mentor, Abraham Adams. The *plot* is best defined as the means by which the author mediates the *story* to his readers. The *structure* refers to the methods by which (and the components from which) the *plot* is assembled.

Story

Two main points arise in connection with the story; both concern its origins in so far as it is not an entirely original invention by Fielding.

(a) Derivation from Pamela. Earlier critics often asserted or implied that *Joseph Andrews* originated in Fielding's desire to have a second satirical bite at Richardson. He is envisaged as starting out with the idea of standing *Pamela* on its head (virtuous footman withstands assaults of lecherous Lady employer) and then, finding that the first few chapters had exhausted the comic potential of this notion, going on to create, almost by accident, the first English picaresque novel. I do not think this stands up to examination. First, *Shamela* was not a damp squib; it was a devastatingly effective parody. Fielding had hit the bullseye first time: there was no need for a second shot. *Joseph Andrews* is not a derivative work. It could not resemble *Pamela* because the idea of the 'comic romance' Fielding sets out in *The Author's Preface* requires a totally different ambience, in particular an 'outdoor' as opposed to an 'indoor' setting. Again, Joseph is not the mere instrument of a sustained joke. Too much trouble is taken to individualise him at the outset; the last thing Fielding should have done if he wished his readers simply to laugh *at* him.

It is *possible* that Adams, and the *Author's Preface* for that matter, may be afterthoughts, but in the absence of any evidence whatever for this hypothesis it must be disregarded. Once the first few chapters have gone by we hear no more of the Booby connection until near the end of Book III. There are subsequent little jabs at Richardson's style and characteristic sentiments from time to time, as there are at Colley Cibber's, but these have nothing to do with the story or the plot. The *negative* influence of *Pamela* on the moral structure is another matter, of course.

(b) Influence of folk-tale. It seems to me quite possible that Fielding drew some of the strands in his plot from the common stock of folk or fairy-tales. He plainly knew them; he mentions *Jack the Giant Killer*, he adapted *Tom Thumb* for the stage. There is not space to go into this theory in detail but, for a start, Joseph, born – apparently – of poor parents, with nothing in his favour save courage and good nature, is the archetypal folk-hero. He is befriended by an old 'magician' (Adams), incurs the enmity of a wicked 'witch' (Lady Booby, who tries to 'cast her spell' upon him), undergoes many 'ordeals' to test his constancy in his 'quest' for the hand of a 'princess in disguise' (Fanny), defeats the 'rivals for her hand' (e.g. Didapper) and is restored to his 'rightful inheritance' by the disclosures of a mysterious old pedlar, also finding his long-lost father, from whom he was stolen while in his cradle by the 'fairies' (gipsies) as was Fanny, of course. I do not suggest a conscious incorporation of this material, of course, rather a sound instinct for what would please an audience very far from sophisticated, for the most part. Folk-tales, after all, often contain quests and nearly always end happily.

Plot and structure

The basic plot is, of course, a journey. In this Fielding follows his acknowledged sources for the 'comic romance'. *Don Quixote* largely comprises the Knight's wanderings in search of chivalrous enterprises. Further in the background lie Homer's *Odyssey* and Virgil's *Aeneid*, both about epic voyages. In the event, however, the journey in *Joseph Andrews* does not subsume the whole novel by any means. Half the first Book, the whole of the last, and – if we include the digressions both long and short – sizeable parts of Books II and III also, are at fixed locations. Nevertheless, and quite apart from precedents, the journeys of Fielding's cast of characters to Booby Hall give the plot what unity it has, as well as offering Fielding a number of advantages in achieving his aims; these are:

(a) *The furtherance of his avowed intention to range through a wide cross-section of different classes and conditions of mankind.* A journey – especially one with frequent halts at wayside inns – provides opportunities for encounters no static situation could have provided, meetings with two contrasted parsons and a Roman Catholic priest for instance, or with three samples of the magistracy.

(b) *The creation of a fictional world as unlike that of Richardson as possible.* Samuel Taylor Coleridge, the famous poet and critic, has a brilliant note on *Tom Jones* that applies just as forcefully to *Joseph Andrews*. He says, 'There is a cheerful, sun-shiny, breezy spirit that prevails everywhere, strongly contrasted with the hot, day-dreamy continuity of Richardson'. We have the open air, movement, the spice of adventure, physical combat. We feel, in Dryden's phrase for Shakespeare, that 'Here is God's plenty'. This is Fielding's natural *métier*; he had none of Richardson's skill in the meticulous dissection of personality, he needed to make his point with verve and force, and then move on.

(c) *The inclusion of some Biblical parallels.* It is sufficiently obvious that Abraham Adams is an appropriate name for a clergyman, but there is more to it than that. Adam was the father of us all, Abraham (in Genesis, XII *et seq.*) is the father of his people who leads them into the land of Canaan and then subsequently out of Egypt into the Negeb, and also delivers his kinsman Lot from the wicked inhabitants of Sodom and Gomorrah. He is also only saved from having to sacrifice his son Isaac by the direct intervention of God, an incident which Adams is made to quote (Book IV, Ch. 7) immediately prior to the point where he is told that *his* son has been drowned, in order to persuade Joseph to submit to Providence. There is a very clear parallel to the Parable of the Good Samaritan (in Book I, Ch. 12). Finally, of course, there is the deliberate parallel with Joseph's biblical namesake and Potiphar's wife (already remarked on in the Commentary). These references would not have escaped the notice of Fielding's contemporaries. They are included to lend weight to the moral points Fielding is making.

(d) *The development of his narrative 'in imitation of the manner of Cervantes'.* It is not merely the similarities between Adams and Don Quixote that Fielding meant by his acknowledgement on the title-page of a debt to *Don Quixote*. Both are big, awkward, badly dressed, both invariably assume good intentions in those they meet. But much more to the point is the allusion to the 'manner' of Cervantes. What Fielding is concerned with is not to 'copy' incidents (though there are resemblances, for example, *Don Quixote*, III, 2, and *Joseph Andrews*, IV, 14), but to attempt the same tone, that of a 'laughing philosopher', using comedy, even farce, to make serious comments on human behaviour. The heroic simplicity of Adams is precisely like that of Don Quixote in this respect, that they are touchstones of the goodness, or the meanness, of everyone they meet. Those who mock, hate or attempt to humiliate them reveal their own unpleasantness in so doing. Those who help and befriend them (albeit they smile at some of their antics) give testimony of their own large-heartedness or, as Fielding would say, charity.

(e) *The employment of classical references for comic purposes.* Fielding cites Homer's supposedly 'lost' comic epic, *The Margites*. Since *Margites* means, roughly speaking, Booby, and since Fielding was a good classical scholar, it is not surprising to find him amusing himself, together with those of his readers who share his educational background, by, for example, parodying the style of translators of the classics, slipping in fragments of Greek and Latin, sometimes with errors included, to show up the ignorance of those who affect to know the classics, sometimes to give credence to his praise of Adams's learning.

Fielding's achievement in the structure of Joseph Andrews. As we have just seen there were a good few precedents for Fielding's choice of a journey for his plot. But there were snags too. The more obvious one has already been pointed out; it is the inherently elastic nature of journeys. They can go on indefinitely; and stopping short with the conventional 'And so they lived happily ever after' is unlikely to satisfy adult readers. Associated with this is the principal weakness of the picaresque novel. One need not necessarily object in principle to the hero's stepping out gaily into the future with his pockets jingling with guineas. The trouble is that such heroes as Gil Blas, or Smollett's Roderick Random who survive, by luck or cunning, all manner of (often richly deserved) misadventures is that they remain, in all essentials, what they were to start with. They don't grow up.

Now Fielding felt that those who learn nothing from experience (like Adams and like Lady Booby) may be either very good or very bad indeed, but are of little help to the rest of us. Joseph is young and impressionable, he ought to be capable of profiting morally from his ups and downs, and we, the readers, ought to be able to learn from him about ourselves, in a different way from that which we learn from the passengers in the stage-coach, Trulliber or Pounce, say. A healthy diet is one thing and a dose of castor oil another. Both, Fielding thought, were necessary at different times for moral health.

The final problem Fielding had to solve in structuring *Joseph Andrews* was how to finish. For it had become, I think, increasingly apparent to Fielding that he could not mark the return of the travellers to Booby Hall with the simplistic formula of reunion and riches all round. The last Book offers instead an elaborately plotted and carefully managed dénouement, marked by the ingenuity with which a number of strands (that have emerged piecemeal during the journey) are first further entangled and then triumphantly unravelled. This winds up the narrative tension to a much higher pitch than before. Accordingly, I shall trace the pattern Fielding followed in Book IV in order to show that there was nothing casual or haphazard about his writing here. Rather it was the result of more conscious design than he had hitherto employed in *Joseph Andrews*.

The catalyst in all the action is Lady Booby. Her renewed love–hate relationship with Joseph is both a prime obstacle to the projected marriage and the occasion of the ultimate test of Adams's integrity, his family's involvement adding a new dimension to his predicament. Her plotting with Scout is more dangerous, because more deliberate, than any of the trials that have previously beset the lovers, but its destruction by the arrival of the newly-wed Boobys clears one problem only to present another. Joseph's newfound social standing not only makes Fanny an 'unsuitable' match but it turns him into a just-feasible husband for Lady Booby. It would be a scandalous but not inconceivable match. Moreover, in Squire Booby and Pamela, or rather in their attitudes, there are further obstacles to the marriage, and their ready acceptance of Joseph offers him a temptation to discard Fanny too. But though Joseph and Adams withstand their testing, the arrival of the pedlar with what we might now call his 'disinformation' deprives Joseph of his power to choose Fanny and throw up his 'position' just as he is making the choice. Fanny too has been offered a temptation, of sorts, in Didapper. The bedroom farce, itself quite complex, adds a possible motive for a breach between Adams and Joseph. With it, the mood of the novel turns sunny again however, thus preparing the ground for the Andrews family's entrance, and the final resolution of the dilemma (not without a last minute hitch or two), with the clinching arrival of Mr Wilson.

To conclude then, *Joseph Andrews* as a whole is not a book about which we can talk very meaningfully in terms of its design. Like many old houses, it perhaps owes a good deal of its attraction to its somewhat higgledy-piggledy nature. Only in Book IV can we call Fielding, by analogy, an architect, a title which, in his next book *Tom Jones*, he eminently deserves. However, Book IV is, in itself, a very satisfying structure and I would conjecture that Fielding's knowledge of the stage led him to set it up as something very like a play. It exhibits the classical 'unities': the significant action all occurs at Booby Hall, the time, up to the climax, is restricted to twenty-four hours, and every occurrence bears upon the narrative in one way or another. The gains in terms of tightness and coherence are marked. Book IV makes a long stride towards the novel as we know it today.

6.3 FIELDING'S STYLE AND USE OF IRONY

In so far as his prose is typical of an age which worked within conventions somewhat different from our own, I have dealt with this aspect of Fielding's craft in Chapter 6.1 (*How to read Joseph Andrews*). But there are some important matters which call for more particular comment, since they contribute to Fielding's originality as an author, to his distinctive artistry. Most contemporary novelists – there are exceptions naturally – tend to employ a uniform style in their works, with the obvious exception of dialogue, where the nature and social class of the speaker determine the language he or she uses, just as they do in Fielding, of course, who is capable of a nice discrimination between mock and true gentility, real learning and pseudo-scholarship, and so on. This 'modern' style is not designed to call attention to itself, it is a 'transparent' style one might say, of which the purpose is to keep the narrative flowing easily, and on no account to interpose the author's personality. To those accustomed to this almost anonymous approach, Fielding's will appear quirky, even eccentric, because – though he can produce this kind of even-paced, low-key narrative when he likes – he has a wide range of manners, and he deploys them at his own preference, changing his style from chapter to chapter, and often from paragraph to paragraph. I shall comment on one or two passages which seem to me to embody many of Fielding's techniques.

Book I, Chapter 8 opens with a flourish. Yet the mock classical nature of the metaphor is immediately given away by such 'vulgarisms' as *rake, breeches* and *housewife* used in the context of Greek deities. There follow two paragraphs of tongue-in-cheek praise of Lady Booby and 'the ladies' who are reading the book. The long, intricate sentences are typical of Fielding's sub-acid, bantering style. Phrases like '*rampant* passion for chastity' '*violent* modesty and virtue' use their adjectives to contradict their overt meaning. This serves as a dry introduction to a perfectly serious, indeed almost 'flat', description of Joseph, only varied by the brilliant twist at the end. Such satirical 'squibs and crackers' to use one of his own phrases, are often introduced without warning to enliven the narrative. Next come two long passages of virtually dramatic dialogue, preceded by a speech by Lady Booby which she intends to be stiffly formal, but in which Fielding contrives to make her give away her true intentions pretty comprehensively. The ironic tone which this introduces is sustained and developed in the dialogue, every phrase of Lady Booby's suggesting, without ever quite admitting, her intentions towards Joseph; every phrase of his politely conveying his incomprehension, until he mentions his 'virtue'.

There follows a magnificently extended mock-epic simile to convey Lady Booby's own incomprehension, her astonishment, which produces a 'silence of two minutes' at Joseph's use of this phrase (which is of course a *leitmotiv* in *Pamela*). The style of this is button-holing and colloquial, a compact parody, with its contemporary references, of true epic simile. Then comes Lady Booby's rage, Joseph's citation of *Pamela* (which as I have said elsewhere sustains the parody at some cost to Joseph's credibility as a character) and finally the first of Lady Booby's soliloquies, artificially phrased so as to guy both its speaker and the literary genre it derives from.

I am not suggesting that Fielding moves jerkily from one style to another; rather he modulates easily into the manner appropriate to his subject matter. His continual shifts of viewpoint, of tone of voice, add both variety and vivacity to this episode, they help to carry the narrative forward and also to retain the reader's interest.

In all this irony is so much the dominant mood that it merits separate consideration, and perhaps, since it is often employed loosely, the word may be defined. Dr Johnson's *Dictionary* of 1747 defines *irony* as 'expressing one thing and meaning another' but, to be effective, the author must somehow ensure that the reader catches on to the covert meaning, and does not simply accept the surface sense. This calls for a reasonably alert reader sometimes, though, in its more elementary forms, Fielding's irony can easily be recognised. So, when Fielding remarks that Mrs Tow-wouse's perception of her husband's dalliance with Betty 'added very little to the natural sweetness of her temper' we at once understand what her *temper* is really like. But the irony may have layers, like an onion. When Fielding writes (of Joseph's defence of his virtue), 'man should rejoice that he cannot, like a poor weak woman, be ravished against his will' there is, uppermost, simple irony (how often do women 'ravish' unwilling men?) next, mockery of *Pamela*, and last, not at all funny, the bitter underlayer of truth.

Then there is what might be called cumulative irony. Thus, the two lawyers' conflicting adulation and vilification of the squire (in Book II, Ch. 3) merely puzzles Adams, and us, until the landlord blows the whistle on the pair of them. A more sustained and complex instance still is found in Book II, Chapter 8, where Adams, with perfect innocence and some naive pride, relates his adventures among politicians, whom he praises with entire sincerity for their generosity and good intentions, though all of them have let him down and none has even attempted to keep his promises to the electors. More examples of Fielding's irony will be found in the commentary. Sometimes, no doubt, he overdoes it. Where he makes fun of Adams's sermonising he runs the risk, as A. E. Dyson has said, of 'sabotaging his own effect'. But, by and large, irony is the device to which he devotes his mastery of style, above all others. There are hints that he *could* do other things well – the idyllic vignette of Book III, Chapter 5 for example. But there is no doubt that the controlling tone of *Joseph Andrews*, for all its frequent explosions of farce, and moments of high seriousness, is ironic. After all, hypocrisy, which affects virtues it does not possess, is best exposed by irony which strips away the verbiage from the truth.

The centrality of irony in *Joseph Andrews* should not blind us to the presence of other qualities in Fielding's prose, of which another prime constituent is what I can best describe as his vivacity. He was exceptionally responsive to the infinite oddities and absurdities of life which go to make man, in Pope's famous phrase, 'The glory, jest and riddle of the world'. Individuality, eccentricity, whimsicality are all relished by a man whose experiences as a magistrate gave him unrivalled opportunities for observing them. The Italian traveller (of Book II, Ch. 5) and the incognito priest (of Book III, Chapter 8), the cynical bookseller, the landlord who has been a sailor, the disputing poet and player, even Miss Grave-airs, are all, strictly speaking, extraneous to the plot. But they all add to the rich, pulsating life of the novel, they are all pictured in vivid thumbnail sketches.

To sum up then, the three major constituents of Fielding's style are its variety, its irony and its vivacity. If, as has been said '*Le style, c'est l'homme même*' (Style is the man himself), then Fielding's conveys his wide ranging, tolerant insight into the follies and graces of mankind, his delight in their vagaries and absurdities, and his sceptical, but never finally despairing, assessment of their aspirations.

7 SPECIMEN PASSAGE
AND ANALYSIS

7.1 SPECIMEN (BOOK I, CH. 12)

The thief who had been knocked down had now recovered himself; and both together fell to belabouring poor Joseph with their sticks, till they were convinced they had put an end to his miserable being: they then stript him entirely naked, threw him into a ditch, and departed with their booty.

The poor wretch, who lay motionless a long time, just began to recover his senses as a stage-coach came by. The postilion, hearing a man's groans, stopt his horses, and told the coachman, He was certain there was a *dead* man lying in the ditch, for he heard him groan. "Go on, sirrah," says the coachman; "we are confounded late, and have no time to look after dead men." A lady, who heard what the postilion said, and likewise heard the groan, called eagerly to the coachman to stop and see what was the matter. Upon which he bid the postilion alight, and look into the ditch. He did so and returned, "That there was a man sitting upright as naked as ever he was born." "O J-sus!" cried the lady;" a naked man! Dear coachman, drive on and leave him." Upon this the gentleman got out of the coach; and Joseph begged them to have mercy upon him; for that he had been robbed and almost beaten to death. "Robbed!" cries an old gentleman: "let us make all the haste imaginable, or we shall be robbed too." A young man who belonged to the law answered, "He wished they had passed by without taking any notice; but that now they might be proved to have been *last in his company*; if he should die, they might be called to some account for his murder. He therefore thought it advisable to save the poor creature's life, for their own sakes, if possible; at least, if he dies, to prevent the jury's finding *that they fled for it*, he was therefore *of opinion* to take the man into the coach, and carry him to the next inn." The lady insisted, "That he should not come into the coach. That if they lifted him in, she would herself alight: for she would rather stay in that place to all eternity than ride with a naked man." The coachman objected, "That he could not suffer him to be taken in, unless someone would pay a shilling for his carriage the four miles." Which the two gentlemen refused to do. But the lawyer, who was afraid of some mischief happening to himself, if the wretch was left behind in that condition, saying no man could be too cautious in these matters, and that he remembered very extraordinary cases in the books, threatened the coachman, and bid him deny taking him up at his peril; for that, if he died, he should be indicted for his murder; and if he lived, and brought an action against him, he would willingly take a brief in it. These words had a sensible effect on the coachman, who was well acquainted with the person who spoke them; and the old gentleman above mentioned, thinking the naked man would afford him frequent opportunities of showing his wit to the lady, offered to join with the company in giving a mug of beer for his fare; till, partly alarmed by the threats of the one, and partly by the promises of the other, and being perhaps a *little* moved with compassion at the poor creature's condition, who stood bleeding and shivering with the cold, he at length agreed; and Joseph was now advancing to the coach, where, seeing the lady, who held the sticks of her fan before her eyes, he absolutely refused, miserable as he was, to enter, unless he was furnished with sufficient covering to prevent giving the least offence to decency. So perfectly modest was this young man; such mighty effects had the spotless example of the amiable Pamela, and the excellent sermons of Mr. Adams, wrought upon him.

Though there were several greatcoats in the coach, it was not easy to get over this difficulty which Joseph had started. The two gentlemen complained that they were cold, and could not spare a rag: the man of wit saying, with a laugh "that charity began at home"; and the coachman, who had two greatcoats under him, refused to lend either, lest they should be made bloody; the lady's footman desiring to be excused for the same reason, which the lady herself, notwithstanding her abhorrence of a naked man, approved; and it is more than probable poor Joseph, who obstinately adhered to his modest resolution, must have perished, unless the postilion (a lad who hath since been transported for robbing a hen-roost) had voluntarily stript off a greatcoat, his only garment, at the same time swearing a great oath (for which he was rebuked by the passengers), "That he would rather ride in his shirt all his life than suffer a fellow creature to lie in so miserable a condition."

Joseph, having put on the greatcoat, was lifted into the coach, which now proceeded on its journey. He declared himself almost dead with the cold, which gave the man of wit occasion to ask the lady, if she could not accommodate him with a dram. She answered with some resentment, "She wondered at his asking her such a question: but assured him she never tasted any such thing."

The lawyer was inquiring into the circumstances of the robbery, when the coach stopt, and one of the ruffians, putting a pistol in, demanded their money of the passengers, who readily gave it them; and the lady, in her fright, delivered up a little silver bottle, of about a half-pint size, which the rogue, clapping it to his mouth, and drinking her health, declared, held some of the best Nantes[1] he had ever tasted: this the lady afterwards assured the company was the mistake of her maid, for that she had ordered her to fill the bottle with Hungary-water.[2]

As soon as the fellows were departed, the lawyer, who had, it seems, a case of pistols in the seat of the coach,[3] informed the company, that if it had been daylight, and he could have come at his pistols, he would not have submitted to the robbery; he likewise set forth that he had often met highwaymen when he travelled on horseback, but none ever durst attack him; concluding, that if he had not been more afraid for the lady than for himself, he should not have now parted with his money so easily.

As wit is generally observed to love to reside in empty pockets, so the gentleman whose ingenuity we have above remarked, as soon as he had parted with his money, began to grow wonderfully facetious. He made frequent allusion to Adam and Eve, and said many excellent things on figs, and fig leaves; which perhaps gave more offence to Joseph than to any other in the company.

The lawyer likewise made several very pretty jests, without departing from his profession. He said, 'If Joseph and the lady were alone, he would be more capable of making a *conveyance*[4] to her, as his *affairs* were not *fettered* with any *incumbrance*: he'd warrant he soon suffered a *recovery* by a writ of *entry*, which was the proper way to create *heirs in tail*; that, for his own part, he would engage to make so *firm a settlement* in a coach, that there should be no danger of an *ejectment*"; with an inundation of the like gibberish, which he continued to vent till the coach arrived at an inn, where one servant-maid only was up, in readiness to attend to the coachman, and furnish him with cold meat and a dram. Joseph desired to alight, and that he might have a bed prepared for him, which the maid readily promised to perform: and, being a good-natured wench, and not so squeamish as the lady had been, she clapt a large fagot on the fire, and, furnishing Joseph with a greatcoat belonging to one of the hostlers, desired him to sit down and warm himself, while she made his bed. The coachman, in the meantime, took an opportunity to call up a surgeon, who lived within a few doors; after which, he reminded his passengers how late they were, and, after they had taken leave of Joseph, hurred them off as fast as he could.

The wench soon got Joseph to bed, and promised to use her interest to borrow him a shirt; but imagined, as she afterwards said, by his being so bloody, that he must be a dead man; she ran with all speed to hasten the surgeon, who was more than half drest, apprehending that the coach had been overturned and some lady or gentleman hurt. As soon as the wench had informed him at his window that it was a poor foot-passenger who had been stripped of all he had, and almost murdered, he chid her for disturbing him so early, slipped off his clothes again, and very quietly returned to bed and to sleep.

Notes

1. *Nantes* = brandy.
2. *Hungary-water* = an innocuous rosemary-flavoured cordial.
3. *Seat of the coach,* i.e. under the driver.
4. *Conveyance, etc.* All these snippets of legal terminology are, of course, capable of bawdy constructions.

7.2 ANALYSIS

This famous passage has been much discussed. You should refer to the comments on it by both Dyson and Battestin (see Further Reading) if possible. In so far as the mechanics of the plot are concerned Fielding needed to expedite a meeting between Joseph and Adams which would also put Adams under the necessity of accompanying Joseph back to Booby Hall, and make Joseph dependent upon his former mentor again. So Joseph is to be discovered, penniless and injured, at an inn. The introductory fight (not quoted here) shows Joseph as brave, though not foolhardy and also reveals the random violence and danger of eighteenth-century travel. The wanton brutality of the robbers is not untypical of men who had nothing to lose (hanging was certain if they were caught, which as Fielding himself argued, made murder all the more likely). But their savagery also closely, and deliberately, echoes the parable of the Good Samaritan (Luke x, verses 30–37) where 'thieves stripped and beat him and departed leaving him half dead'.

At this point Fielding makes the parable more topical by bringing a coach upon the scene, at the same time widening the range of selfishness on show from the Priest and the Levite who 'passed by on the other side' in the original. Although the postilion (who rode upon one of the lead horses, as is still done today on the Royal State Coach) is presented humorously he is genuinely concerned, unlike his master the coachman, who is concerned only with his job. So, as a first irony, it is only the idle curiosity of the 'lady' which causes Joseph's rescue. His nakedness changes her mind (there is a sharp reminder of the Gospels in her cry of 'O Jesus') so that the gentlemen's interest is also aroused. Joseph's appeal that they should 'have mercy upon him' employs a phrase that they would all be accustomed to repeat every Sunday in the Prayer

Book responses to the Ten Commandments (or to Jesus's summary of them, concluding 'Thou shalt love thy neighbour as thyself' which, in answer to the query 'Who is my neighbour?' prompted him to tell the parable of the Good Samaritan). The appeal has no effect at all, for all its overtones.

Each passenger has a reason for abandoning Joseph and all are totally egotistic. But just as self-centred is the lawyer's motive for urging them to take Joseph in, a brilliant stroke of acrid irony. The lady now affects modesty, the coachman duty, the gentlemen, presumably, poverty, until they are all frightened by the lawyer's threats. They then, reluctantly, change their minds, the lawyer having merely substituted one kind of selfishness for another. (It was, incidentally, a lawyer to whom Jesus related the parable of the Samaritan in the first place.) The picture of the lawyer, with his scraps of legal jargon, is acidulated, the three 'gentlemen' – so-called – are alike in their miserliness, but the masterstroke is Fielding's superbly timed and positioned final clause in the long sentence which shows the coachman gradually weakening ' . . . perhaps a *little* moved with compassion at the poor creature's condition, who stood bleeding and shivering with the cold'. The vision of Joseph as an anonymous 'poor creature' points up, with Swiftian ferocity, the absence in the passengers of any claim to humanity. The collective heartlessness, the bland self-regard of a representative cross-section of society faced with utter destitution and serious injury, is clinched by the sheer hypocrisy of the lady who, by holding the *sticks* of her fan (when opened it was possible to see through these) gets a good view of the naked man, rather than see whom she *says* she would 'stay in that place to all eternity'. It is perhaps a pity, as it is certainly superfluous, for Fielding to have inserted a dig at Pamela.

The next paragraph is the climactic one in Fielding's version of the parable. The picture of collective self-absorption is made even more vitriolic by the bland matter of fact way Fielding relates it. He never allows his voice to become shrill in the whole chapter and the passengers' evasions sound almost reasonable until we come to the postilion's emergence as the one and only representative of charity in the coach. This brings the episode to a peak, just as we recall that the biblical equivalent of the postilion, the Samaritan himself, belonged to a despised and downtrodden ethnic group. We notice the deadly thrusts in parenthesis (transported for robbing a *hen roost*), 'his *only* garment', '*rebuked* by the passengers'. As Fielding turns the screw of his contempt ever tighter the passengers become ever more contemptible.

Stylistically, the whole passage is notable for the way in which its long, swift-flowing sentences each build up to a withering or a disgusted climax.

The reappearance of the robbers exposes the affectation as well as the tight-fistedness of the lady (and half a pint is a lot of brandy!) The lawyer's cowardice, bravado and glib self-justification are underlined again. His 'jokes' – quite untypical of Fielding in their smuttiness and lack of geniality – add a further dimension of nastiness and triviality to the scene. (Fielding signifies his contemptuous view of this kind of 'wit' by the words *gibberish* and *vent up*. He had, no doubt, heard more than enough of it in legal circles.)

In the remainder of the chapter the same themes are reiterated, but with variations to drive home the satiric points yet further. Thus it is Betty the 'good-natured' (something of a key word in Fielding) and the amicable Mr Tow-wouse who now take on the role of samaritan, neither of whom is – in another and narrower sense – a model of 'virtue'. Indeed, the two might be described as examples of those 'publicans and sinners' whom Jesus was accused of spending his time with by the Pharisees. It is evident that wealth and rank, rather than any sense of a duty to the sick, motivate the surgeon. But, now we are at the inn, comedy has re-entered, Mrs Tow-wouse is a monster it is true, but we are meant to laugh at her. The coach, on the other hand, contains nothing truly comic. It is, quite literally, hell on wheels.

8 CRITICAL RECEPTION

In 1741 there were no newspapers as we know them and such outlets as then existed for reviewing literature regarded the novel as beneath notice for the most part. For anything strictly contemporary we must rely on private letters, though we know *Joseph Andrews* sold quickly and the names of its characters soon passed into common use. Thomas Gray the poet (1716–1771) writing to his friend Richard West in 1741 said,

> The characters have a great deal of nature, which always pleases even in the lowest shapes. Parson Adams is perfectly well and so is Mrs Slipslop . . . His reflections upon high people and low people . . . are very good.

Yet the Abbé Desfontaines, writing in a French review (where novels were more highly regarded) enthused. 'It is a judicious and moral novel, full of salt and pleasures . . . and is infinitely interesting.' (He went on to translate it in 1744.) But there is really very little to go on.

Later, however, after the publication of *Tom Jones*, a critical dispute blew up over the relative merits of Richardson and Fielding which has continued, intermittently, ever since. Dr Samuel Johnson may speak for Richardson since, though he was unfair to Fielding (and had not, he said, read *Joseph Andrews*) he does discriminate nicely between the two authors in general terms. He said that in their novels there was '. . . all the difference between the characters of nature and the characters of manners ' (we might paraphrase this as 'realistic' and 'stylised'). Richardson was a man 'who knew how a watch was made' while Fielding 'could tell the time by looking at the dial plate'. He also told his biographer, Boswell, that 'there was more knowledge of the heart in one letter of Richardson's (i.e. in *Clarissa*) than in all *Tom Jones*, which he thought a 'vicious book', according to his friend Mrs Piozzi. Johnson was an acute critic, bothered by the 'immorality' of *Tom Jones*, though he read *Amelia* at one sitting and admired it. Boswell, though he recorded these strictures in his *Life of Johnson*, dissented so strongly that he felt obliged to defend Fielding, as 'ever favourable to honour and honesty' and 'cherishing the benevolent and generous affections'.

Nevertheless Johnson has a point, and his distinction between 'nature' and 'manner' is undeniably valid. After all he might have quoted Fielding himself in *Joseph Andrews* (Book III, Ch. 1) where he stresses his determination to deal 'not with men but with manners, not with an individual but a species'. Fielding and Richardson were pursuing different objectives. No attempt is made in *Joseph Andrews* to 'dive into the human heart' as Johnson put it. But this proves nothing at all about relative worth unless we assume that superficiality attaches to Fielding's approach, and profundity to Richardson's. Johnson's own test of a writer's outlasting a century if he were to attain 'classical' status has been passed by Fielding with flying colours. The great historian Gibbon said *Tom Jones* 'would survive the Imperial Eagle of the House of Austria' and it has.

When we come to the great Victorian novelists they almost all revere Fielding (though Charlotte Brontë and George Eliot are exceptions, both finding Fielding stronger meat than they could stomach). This is, of course, an aspect of Fielding – his abrasive masculinity – that has often been objected to. Amidst the growing prudery of mid-Victorian England, Thackeray said Fielding was the 'last English novelist' to be allowed to portray 'a man'. But Dickens and Trollope both admired him, and Sir Walter Scott, in his *Lives of the Novelists* had earlier written of him as the 'father of the English novel . . . in his powers of strong and national humour, and forcible yet natural exhibition of character, unapproached as yet . . .' That was written in 1821 however. By the 1860s Trollope was having to alter 'fat stomach' to 'chest' in one of his novels, and Fielding was relegated to the locked bookcase as unsuitable for 'young persons'.

In fact his unpopularity with the Victorians, or some of them, arose from that very kind of prudish affectation which he derides in *Joesph Andrews* (*via* the lady with the fan in the stage coach). However, by the 1890s the more extreme prudery was on the decline, and the publication of a scholarly edition of all his works, edited by the poet W. E. Henley in sixteen volumes, heralded a revival. George Saintsbury in his study, *The Peace of the Augustans* and in the perceptive introductions he wrote for editions of the novels, made high claims for *Joseph Andrews*, writing of 'the sublime, the unprecedented, the rarely equalled and never surpassed figure of Parson Adams', and others echoed him, Thomas Hardy, for one, acknowledging Fielding's influence. But a new conception of the novel, one much more akin to Richardson's than to Fielding's was beginning to gain ground by this time, and between the two wars Fielding's literary reputation, though he was never out of print or unread, was at a low ebb. V. S. Pritchett, in his fine essay *The Ancestor* (see Further Reading) acted as devil's advocate; '[Fielding] is said to be that most tiresome of bores, the man's man. He sets up as the shallowest of philosophers, the man of the world, whose world turns out to be a box of tricks. His geniality labours the offence'. His own repudiation of these charges is devastating but the strictures of F. R. Leavis, who excluded Fielding from what he called '*The Great Tradition*' (along with Hardy and nearly all of Dickens) were influential, though perfunctory and question-begging to the last degree. The best answer to Leavis is 'In Defence of Fielding' by Middleton Murry (see Further Reading). He tackles Leavis with gusto and point, making an admirable case for Fielding as a writer of 'moral conviction' who believed there was a 'generosity of the body' as well as of the mind, and his conclusion will do for mine too. He says:

[To Fielding] self-regarding egoism, no matter what uniform of respectability it carries, was hateful; solicitude for others, no matter how disreputably arrayed, was to be loved.

This might very well serve as an epigraph for *Joseph Andrews*.

REVISION QUESTIONS

1. 'There is really no plot to speak of in *Joseph Andrews*; one thing leads to another, that is all.' Do you agree?

2. By discussing two or three brief episodes attempt to show how each contributes something to the themes Fielding is treating in the book as a whole.

3. Fielding said it was his intention to expose 'affectation'. Illustrate some of the varying methods he employs for this purpose.

4. *Joseph Andrews* is, according to E. M. Forster, 'interesting as an example of a false start'. How far do you agree, if at all?

5. What do you understand by the phrase 'Fielding's moral vision' as applied to *Joseph Andrews*?

6. How far can the term 'picaresque' be usefully applied to *Joseph Andrews*?

7. Fielding intended to write *Joseph Andrews* 'in the manner of Cervantes'. Discuss the importance of *Don Quixote* and other literary influences upon *Joseph Andrews*.

8. '*Joseph Andrews* would have been a better book without the recurrent mockery of Richardson's *Pamela*. It gets in the way of what Fielding wanted to say.' Discuss.

9. 'Parson Adams is to Joseph Andrews as the sun is to the solar system. Without him, everything is cold and lifeless.' Discuss.

10. 'By making fun of Adams Fielding calls in question his own seriousness about the things Adams stands for.' Do you agree?

11. 'The hero and heroine are failures; Joseph is too good to be true, Fanny a pretty face and an empty head.' Discuss.

12. Discuss Fielding's treatment of any *three* of the following: Lady Booby, Mrs Slipslop, Peter Pounce, Justice Frolick, the Tow-wouses, Mr Wilson.

13. Discuss some of the methods Fielding employs to move us to 'exquisite mirth and laughter'.

14. 'Irony is the predominant technique by which Fielding exposes hypocrisy'. Discuss with examples.

15. 'The taste for horse-play is immature and tiresome'. Is it?

FURTHER READING

(PB = available in paperback, * = strongly recommended)

Texts

The PB editions of *Joseph Andrews* published by Penguin, Dent (Everyman) and Signet (USA) are all sensibly introduced and annotated. However, M. C. Battestin's edition (Methuen, 1961) is by far the best text for study because (a) it has a very full and thorough introduction, (b) it includes the whole of *Shamela*, (c) it is comprehensively annotated. It should at least be consulted. The new Wesleyan edition (OUP) has only textual notes.

Biography

J. Butt, *Fielding** (Writers and their Work) (Longman, 1954) PB is a brilliant sketch.

E. Jenkins, *Henry Fielding** (Home and Van Thal, 1947) is a brief, lively biography.

Criticism

Books

H. Macallister, *Fielding** (Literature in Perspective) (Evans, 1967) PB is an excellent, succinct critical biography. Two good chapters on *Joseph Andrews*.

M. C. Battestin, *The Moral Basis of Fielding's Art* (Connecticut, USA) is a very full and detailed study, concentrating on *Joseph Andrews*. (For selective study.)

A. Wright, *Henry Fielding, Mask and Feast** (Longman, 1965). Two probing chapters.

R. Paulson (ed.), *Fielding. A Collection of Critical Essays* (Prentice-Hall, 1962) PB. contains essays on *Joseph Andrews* by M. Mack* and M. Spilka.*

Essays and articles

For early views see Paulson and Lockwood (eds), *Fielding, The Critical Heritage* (Routledge, 1969). See also the following:

W. Allen, *The English Novel* (Penguin, 1958) PB.

S. T. Coleridge, *Essays and Lectures on Shakespearce, etc.* (Dent: Everyman).

A. E. Dyson, *The Crazy Fabric** (Macmillan, 1966) PB.

W. C. Hazlitt, *Lectures on the English Comic Writers* (Dent: Everyman).

A. Kettle, *An Introduction to the English Novel* (Hutchinson, 1951) PB.

M. Murray, *Unprofessional Essays** (Cape, 1963).

V. S. Pritchett, *The Living Novel** (Chatto, 1946).

Sir Walter Scott, *Lives of the Novelists* (Dent: Everyman).

I. Watt, *The Rise of the Novel* (Penguin, 1963) PB.

Background

D. Taylor, *Fielding's England* (Dobson, 1966).

P. Rogers (ed.), *The Eighteenth Century* (Contexts of English Literature) (Methuen,1978).

B. Willey, *The Eighteenth Century Background* (Chatto, 1965).

Fielding's other novels are readily available in similar editions to *Joseph Andrews*. Richardson's *Pamela* is available in Dent's (Everyman) edition, in two volumes.

Note. Works not in print should be available in public/academic libraries.